RESOURCE BOOKS FOR TEACHERS

series editor
ALAN MALEY

VOCABULARY

John Morgan &
Mario Rinvolucri

Oxford University Press

Oxford University Press
Great Clarendon Street, Oxford OX2 6DP

Oxford New York
Auckland Bangkok Buenos Aires Cape Town Chennai
Dar es Salaam Delhi Hong Kong Istanbul Karachi Kolkata
Kuala Lumpur Madrid Melbourne Mexico City Mumbai Nairobi
São Paulo Shanghai Singapore Taipei Tokyo Toronto

with an associated company in Berlin

Oxford and *Oxford English* are trade marks of
Oxford University Press

ISBN 0 19 437091 7

© Oxford University Press 1986

First published 1987
Fifteenth impression 2002

Set by Katerprint Co. Ltd, Oxford

Printed in China

Acknowledgements

We should like to thank the following people:

students from Davies's and the New School Cambridge, and from Pilgrims, Canterbury; the many colleagues who have supplied us with ideas, who are individually acknowledged where possible; our families, for their participation in writing and testing; writers and publishers who have allowed us to use texts that fall within their copyright:

Douglas Adams and Pan Books for an extract from *The Hitch-Hiker's Guide to the Galaxy* (1979); Associated Newspapers for a news item from the *Daily Mail*; Alan Bold and Macdonald Publishers for 'Cause and Effect', from *In This Corner: Selected Poems 1963–83* (1983); Duncan Campbell and Michael Joseph for an extract from *The Unsinkable Aircraft Carrier* (1984); Paul Christopherson for an extract from *Second Language Learning* (Penguin 1973); Keith Devlin for 'How Archimedes' Number Came Up' (*The Guardian*, 21.6.84); *The Guardian* for three news items; Sheila Hocken and Victor Gollancz for an extract from *Emma and I* (1977); International Distillers and Vintners and Oxford University Press for an advertisement for Smirnoff Vodka (text taken from *The Concise Oxford Dictionary*, 7th edition, 1982); Colin Johnson and Angus and Robertson for an extract from *Wild Cat Falling* (1965); H. R. Kohl and Methuen and Company for an extract from *Writing, Maths and Games* (1977); R. D. Laing, A. Esterson, and Tavistock Publications for an extract from *Sanity and Madness in the Family*; Clarice Maizell for 'A Little Old Thief' (*The Guardian*, 19.12.83); Roger McGough for 'There's Something Sad', from *Penguin Modern Poets 10: The Mersey Sound* (1967); V. S. Naipaul for an extract from *Guerrillas* (Andre Deutsch, 1975); Andrea Newman and Triton Books for an extract from *A Bouquet of Barbed Wire* (1969; currently available in hardback from Inner Circle Books, and in paperback from Penguin); *The New Statesman* for a word game (28.10.83); Julius Nyerere and Oxford University Press for an extract from *Ujamaa* (1968); *The Observer* for 'Great Glasgow Ice-Cream War' (29.4.84) (*The Observer* publishes a resource service for teachers of EFL; in the course of a year's subscription over 150 newspaper articles are prepared, with special exercises and worksheets in a specially designed pack with permission to photocopy; details from The Observer EFL Service, 8 St Andrew's Hill, London EC4V 5JA); Cedric Robinson and David Charles for an extract from *Sand Pilot of Morecambe Bay* (1980); Times Newspapers for 'Charlie Cairoli the Clown Dies Aged 70' (*The Times*, 18.2.80), and 'Redskins Bite the Dust in Tomato War' (*The Sunday Times*, January 1980); the estate of J. R. R. Tolkien and George Allen and Unwin for an extract from *Smith of Wootton Major* (1967); Terry Winograd and Addison-Wesley (Reading, Massachusetts) for an extract from *Language as a Cognitive Process* (1983).

Contents

Section B: Working with texts

B/1	Customizing a text	Intermediate – Advanced	20–30	Choose text and words; make copies of word list ('Air Bases')	30
B/2	Where else do they fit?	Intermediate – Advanced	30–45	Choose text, make copies, select words ('The Towel')	31
B/3	Correct the teacher	Elementary – Advanced	25–35 (1) 45–60 (2)	Choose text, make copies; select words, make cards	33
B/4	On the walls	Beginner – Elementary	15	Assemble posters, maps, etc; translate words	34
B/5	Tape montage	Intermediate – Advanced	15	Make 3–4 minute tape montage	35
B/6	A memory game	Intermediate – Advanced	15–25	Choose text, make copies; select words ('Smith of Wootton Major')	35
B/7	Two-language texts	Beginner – Elementary	15	Prepare text, make copies ('The Barbarians')	36
B/8	Hunt the misfits	Intermediate – Advanced	20–35	Prepare text, make copies ('Charlie Cairoli'; 'Viaduct Rescue')	38
B/9	Ghost definitions	Elementary – Intermediate	20	Choose text, make copies; select words and definitions ('Crossing Morecambe Bay')	40
B/10	Please do not read this notice!	Elementary – Advanced	20–40	Choose text, make copies; select words. Coloured pens ('What is a word?')	41
B/11	Scrambled lines	Elementary – Advanced	15–30	Prepare texts, make copies ('Torrey Canyon'; 'A Railway Worker'; 'Mrs Lily Townsend')	42
B/12	Find the swapped words	Intermediate – Advanced	45–60	Prepare texts, make copies ('Language Manufacture')	44
B/13	Who said what?	Intermediate – Advanced	15–30	Prepare texts, make copies ('State'; 'Society')	46
B/14	Patchwork text	Elementary – Advanced	20–40	Several poetry anthologies	47
B/15	The words in your past	Elementary – Advanced	20–30	Choose text, make copies ('Daddy')	48
B/16	Cross-associations	Elementary – Advanced	15–25	Choose text, make copies ('Goblins')	49
B/17	Keyword diagrams	Elementary – Advanced	15–25	Choose poems, make copies	50
B/18	Be someone else	Intermediate – Advanced	30–40	Choose text, make copies ('The Prince Albert')	51

Section C: Pictures and mime

Section F: Dictionary exercises and word games

Section G: Revision exercises

The authors
and series editor

John Morgan has worked in EFL since 1966, as a teacher, teacher trainer, coursebook and resource book writer, and lexicographer. He has been associated with Pilgrims English Language courses since 1975. With Mario Rinvolucri he has written *Once Upon a Time* and *The Q Book*, as well as contributing to many Pilgrims publications. At present he divides his time between teacher training and setting crosswords.

Mario Rinvolucri currently works for Pilgrims Language Courses as a language teacher, teacher trainer, and writer of EFL ideas books. He is also consultant to the Pilgrims-Longman Teachers' Resource Book series. One of his first EFL books was *Challenge to Think* (with Berer and Frank, OUP, 1982). More recently he has published *Video* (with Cooper and Lavery, 1991) and *Letters* (with Burbridge, Gray, and Levy, 1996) in this series.

Alan Maley worked for The British Council from 1962 to 1988, serving as English Language Officer in Yugoslavia, Ghana, Italy, France, and China, and as Regional Representative in South India (Madras). From 1988 to 1993 he was Director-General of the Bell Educational Trust, Cambridge. From 1993 to 1998 he was Senior Fellow in the Department of English Language and Literature of the National University of Singapore. He is currently a freelance consultant and Director of the Graduate Programme at Assumption University, Bangkok. He has written *Literature,* in the series, *Beyond Words, Sounds Interesting, Sounds Intriguing, Words, Variations on a Theme,* and *Drama Techniques in Language Learning* (all with Alan Duff), *The Mind's Eye* (with Françoise Grellet and Alan Duff), *Learning to Listen* and *Poem into Poem* (with Sandra Moulding, *The Language Teacher's Voice* and *Short and Sweet.* He is also Series Editor for the Oxford Supplementary Skills series.

Foreword

It is curious to reflect that so little importance has been given to vocabulary in modern language teaching. Both the behaviourist/structural model and the functional/communicative model have, in their different ways, consistently underplayed it.

And yet, as any learner of a foreign language knows only too well, words are essential, and the lack of them leads to feelings of insecurity. 'I gotta use words', as the poet says.

How then are words to be had? This book suggests some ways of opening up vocabulary for learners. The authors have based their work on a set of powerful intuitions about how vocabulary is acquired. They could be summarized as follows. The acquisition of vocabulary is

- not a linear but a branching process. Words are not learnt mechanically as little packets of meaning, but associatively.
- not an impersonal but an intensely personal process, therefore. The associations and vibrations that a word sets up depend on our own past and present felt experience.
- not a solitary but a social process. We expand our apprehension of word meanings by interchanging and sharing them with others.
- not a purely intellectual, effortful process but an experiential, 'hands on' process too. An over-intellectual approach causes the language to be seen as object, rather than to be incorporated within the subject—the learner.

The authors, who already have a reputation for creating innovative language teaching materials, have used these insights to produce a set of practical techniques which should be of use to teachers and teacher trainers alike.

Alan Maley

Introduction

To the Anglo-Saxons a vocabulary was a 'wordhoard', to be owned and treasured; to the Chinese, a sea of words to be fished. How do you see your own vocabulary? Which of these words best captures that image?

stock	*tightrope*	*nursery*	*store*	*perimeter*	*pool*
repertoire	*raft*	*armoury*	*palette*	*file*	*mine*
archive	*reservoir*	*web*	*treasury*	*forest*	*tunnel*
spectrum	*orchestra*	*well*	*mountain*	*reserve*	*theatre*
field	*larder*	*tool-kit*	*wardrobe*	*sieve*	*telescope*

What words come to your mind when you see the word *vocabulary*? Write some of them down. Now pronounce the word 'vocabulary'— what other words come to mind? Ask a colleague to do the same: compare your answers.

This book proposes practical exercises to help students learn words: it is neither a book of semantics nor a vocabulary source book. We have avoided presenting 'word fields' ('words to do with laying a table', 'verbs of walking and running'), and concentrate instead on the learning process itself, and on techniques that can be used directly in the classroom. The texts and other materials included may be used by learners, but are intended primarily as exemplification: all of the exercises can be applied to the learning of words wherever encountered, whether in reading, in listening work, or in the process of trying to express oneself.

Why this book?

In 1980, during the hey-day of the 'functional approach' in the UK, we interviewed students in a Cambridge school about their feelings on vocabulary learning. Two thirds of them said they were not taught enough words in class, words they needed when talking to people, watching TV, and reading. They felt their teachers were very keen on teaching them grammar and on improving their pronunciation, but that learning words came a poor third. Later, when we offered a 'vocabulary option' on our Pilgrims courses in Kent, it was flooded with eager students.

Why should this be so? When we 'do' a reading passage or a listening comprehension with our students, surely we *are* teaching vocabulary? Sadly, in many classrooms this is not the case. Encountering and 'understanding' a word are seldom enough: as with meeting people, there need to be depth and interaction for the encounter to be memorable.

Some students recognize this need even where their teachers do not, and develop their own learning systems. A Turkish engineer told us how each day he viewed and audio-recorded the 6 p.m. TV news. He would listen to the recording, pick out all the unfamiliar words and transcribe them, then look them up in an English–English dictionary and from the definitions provide his own Turkish translations. At 9 p.m. he would listen to the news again, and hear many of the words in the same or a slightly modified context. Finally he tested himself next morning, using his bilingual list, covering up first one side and then the other.

A Breton colleague told us that when he was a student he collected new foreign words in match-boxes. He had two match-boxes, one for properly known words and one for unknown or hazy ones. Every now and then he would go through the 'Known' box and check that he still knew all the words. Those he failed on were transferred to the 'Unknown' box. Any words he could recognize in the 'Unknown' box were put in the 'Known' box.

Both of these learners recognized something that their teachers did not: for learning to be effective, attention must be paid to *the student's own process of learning*. This book has grown out of our attempts to work with that process.

A relationship with words

When one is learning a foreign language, many things can get in the way of learning. People have strong, often unexpressed, feelings towards words. Which of these words for *house* do you prefer? Number them in order of preference:

  oikos, casa, hus, ev, haus, ty, spiti, dom, stepi, domus, maison

All sorts of things may have influenced you: the sound you imagined; the look of the word on the page; feelings about the language; the fact that your house may recently have been damaged by an earthquake; the fact that you once used that word wrongly and got laughed at by a native speaker . . .

We conceive of vocabulary learning as a relational process; it could be described as *making friends with the words of the target language*. Why is it, for example, that a learner will immediately remember one word apparently effortlessly, while another met at the same hour will be refused a place in her mind? Don't we sift people and faces in the same mysterious way? Just as a look, a movement, a chance remark, a tone of voice, or something in the setting can influence our first impressions of a person, so can our perception of words be affected by, for example,

– the sounds of the word
– the kinetic sensation of lungs, throat, mouth, and nose (try saying the word *Xhosa*, producing the click that the /x/ represents)

- the shape on a page, on a poster, in the sky, on a TV screen or VDU
- conventional associations: semantic and syntactic categories to which a word is seen to belong, collocations, metaphors, etc.
- literary associations
- the associations the word has for *you* (e.g. what comes to mind when you think of your own name or the name of a street you once lived in?)
- the circumstances of meeting the word (and not just the narrow 'context' of text or utterance, but the room, the people present, the time of day, etc.).

All these factors will play a part in 'learning' a word.

Meanings

Many of the exercises in this book encourage the learner to explore and discuss meanings at a deeper, more personal level than in traditional vocabulary activities. For adequate, motivated learning to take place, we have to go beyond the descriptive frame of lexicography and semantics: the 'dictionary meaning' is only a first step.

Paulo Freire (*Cultural Action for Freedom*, Penguin Books 1972) discovered this when using 'power words' in literacy work: before 'teaching' a word, he would first discover which words used in the community meant most to the learners, and then work outwards from these. In the same way, in *Teacher* (Secker and Warburg 1963), Sylvia Ashton-Warner describes how she taught Maori six-year-olds to read by asking them to tell her words they thought were important enough to learn. (She would put these personal key words on cards for them to take home. If the words were really key words, they really knew them next morning. One child asked for *kick/first mummy/second mummy/knife*, a long way from the feel of the *Janet and John* books, or many EFL coursebooks.)

Words in the classroom

Many of us, like our Turkish student, were forced to work alone. One valuable effect of putting aside classroom time for vocabulary is the opportunity it gives for co-operative learning: sharing and discussing one's learning is far more motivating—and far more *memorable*—than grimly working away on one's own. For the same reason, many of the activities proposed place the teacher in the wings: group work and the classroom reference library play a central role. And again, neighbours and books may be more friendly to learn from than a dominant teacher who towers over the learner.

In constructing pair and group activities, we have been aware that their real importance is often to allow language students to explore new parts of their experience *through* the foreign language. This is why we have tried to find exercises that are new, unexpected and, in a sense, strange. Some teachers will be offended by this strangeness. They will feel that things should be left at a more ordinary and straightforward level. We would argue that language may best be learnt incidentally to substantive cognitive and emotional learning, as was the case when we learned our mother tongue. Second-language learning should not be a stale re-mapping of territories already mapped in great detail through the mother tongue. The learner needs to have the chance to explore radically new territories via the foreign language. This will give the language used a hint of the depth of mastery we possess in the native tongue.

A word to our colleagues

This book does not offer a definitive set of vocabulary learning techniques: since the first collection of our ideas was published in 1980 in *Learning English Words* (Pilgrims Publications, Canterbury), we have learnt a wealth of new ideas from our students and colleagues, and others have come through reading and from personal experience. We hope those who read this book will develop their own store of ideas. If you would like to share them, please write to us at Pilgrims, 8 Vernon Place, Canterbury, Kent CT1 3YG, UK. As teachers, we need to use innovative, stimulating exercises for our own pleasure and renewal as much as for our students' benefit. To ask students to do mediocre, shallow, barely communicative exercises once is boring: to repeat this year after year is soul-destroying for the teacher.

To teachers of other languages

Though this book happens to be in English and gives examples in English, the techniques it contains can be readily adapted for the teaching of any language.

How to use this book

This is a resource book of ideas for teachers and learners. It should be dipped into, not worked through: the division into sections is intended to reflect the styles of activity rather than any progression. As such, it is arbitrary. Sections A and B deal with vocabulary in written texts. Section C exploits the associative power of image and gesture. Section D looks at words in sets: but rather than look at 'word fields' or other predetermined categories, learners are invited to build categories and responses to categories for themselves. Section E explores personal responses to words, from 'life keywords' (E/4) to our feelings about names (E/2). Section F gives ideas for using dictionaries and other reference books in creative, game-oriented ways. Finally, Section G provides activities that can be used to revise words already 'learnt'.

Typically, vocabulary work is woven into the syllabus as and when the student (or more often the teacher) wants or needs it. We hope that the ideas presented here may add to the variety of that work. Alternatively, a portion of each day, or each week, might be set aside: on some intensive language programmes, for example, a 'lexical option' is offered. In either case, the words to be studied would be for the students and you to choose. We have simply offered you frames to fill with the language that you and they want.

In **Section A** you will find a dozen ideas for ways of treating vocabulary before the students meet it in a reading text. So, for example, A/3 is a prediction exercise in which students are told what type of text they are going to read and are asked to predict ten key words they would expect to find in it. These exercises focus students' attention on either new or known vocabulary and at the same time stimulate a desire to find out what is actually in the text. They offer a psychological reason for reading. At the same time it is important to remember that Section A is aimed at helping students broaden and deepen their work on vocabulary—not at furthering good reading habits. Arguably pre-text work on vocabulary focuses students on details in the text, which is not useful in terms of reading strategies.

In **Section B** you will find vocabulary exercises to be done in the course of reading. Again, this is about learning words and *not* about improving reading skills: there are other excellent books that cover this area, for example *Quartet* (Oxford University Press 1982). For our purposes, indeed, the texts may be subordinated to the vocabulary content.

Many of the example materials in this section have been specially written or 'treated' in some way. For example, B/7 presents a mixed-language text aimed at a student who is a beginner in the target language. The target-language words have been carefully selected so as to be easy to guess from context. Thus the student independently begins to learn target-language vocabulary. Again, in B/8 and B/11 the student is shown a passage in which the words have been misplaced, twisted, or messed up, e.g. 'The king and his bean sat down on their thrones side by side'. The students have to edit as they read, in the sentence above replacing *bean* with *queen*. There is power and satisfaction in correcting a foreign reading passage when you are at the lower-intermediate stage of learning. This exercise is one of a family that foster confident, self-reliant, aggressive reading of the foreign language.

In Sections A and B we have offered example texts that you can use to try new ideas out with. Our hope is that you will transfer the techniques that you find work well for you and your students to supplement work on the dialogues and passages in your textbook.

Section C is concerned with the imagery of words. In your textbook, you are provided with umpteen pictures, and most training courses encourage you to make your own library of magazine pictures to teach structures and vocabulary. One of our suggestions (C/3) is that students can produce their own pictures as the frame for learning new words. In this exercise a 'Picasso' comes to the board and draws a picture with the help of the class, while a 'secretary', also supported by the other students, tries to name and label its various parts. The teacher supplies words where the group is stuck.

Students tend to remember what they have created and discovered for themselves. An example of this is C/2: tell your students you would like them to draw all the linking things they can think of. Give two examples: a hinge and a wedding ring. Once they have drawn a dozen things, you ask them to label them in English. They will need dictionaries. They then go round and teach the new words they have found to their classmates. In this exercise the students choose the words they are going to learn and teach. Not everybody will have learnt the same words by the end of the lesson.

Section D looks at the ways we categorize words internally: thematically (D/4); in causative or temporal chains (D/6); through associations that derive from reading or cliché (D/7), prejudice (D/12), or background (D/15). D/16 links the way we view words to our perception of other people, and D/1, D/2, and D/10 show the added meanings that can be created by arbitrary or even perverse categorizations: what items, for example, can *you* think of that are *grey*, *expensive*, and *dangerous*?

In **Section E** the learner is encouraged to explore personal responses to words: E/4 and E/6, for example, give the learner an opportunity to work on the most important words from his or her life experience—the 'power words' that may promote or block learning. In E/3 and E/8, words become both the subject and the content of the discussion.

Section F suggests ways in which the dictionary (and other reference books) can be used as a creative learning aid. There are ideas here for composition (F/9, F/10), finding one's way around reference books (F/1, F/5, F/7), and interactive dictionary games (F/2, F/6, F/12).

'I never let students use a dictionary' is a phrase we have heard thundered across a number of staffrooms. Banning bilingual dictionaries in foreign-language classrooms is almost as absurd as a language teacher trying to mime the meaning of a word like *although* to avoid the cardinal sin of translation back into the students' mother tongue. Dictionaries and translation both have a place in learning.

Section G: The traditional way for students to store vocabulary is in long bilingual lists. Does this ring a bell with you?

puer	*boy*
puella	*girl*
igitur	*therefore*
id	*it*

A friend of ours in Berlin, a computer expert, has now transferred the bilingual list idea to his microcomputer: he stores foreign-language vocabulary on diskette rather than in a notebook. The computer allows him to test himself easily. (A similar program is *Wordstore*, by Chris Jones, Wida Software.) Impossible to imagine a more traditional use of a modern gadget.

Section G proposes a lot of other ways in which students can usefully store words in their vocabulary books, and offers novel and traditional ways of coping with vocabulary revision. So G/5 invites them to draw a ground plan of their flat or house and then to put the words to be revised in appropriate places on the plan. Where would you place these words: *manager/promotion/outperform/climb/compete/disenchanted/memo/errors*? Again, G/2 asks the student to associate words with shapes: circles, triangles, squares, etc. Since there is obviously no 'correct' way of doing this for a given set of words, there is room for student discussion after the categorization has been done individually. It is the talking about the words that anchors them and makes them permanent. When the student comes to revise the words before an end-of-year exam, the words and the shapes on the vocabulary book page bring back interesting memories of interaction—more than can be said for most bilingual lists.

A final word

We feel that a word in isolation from a text is not in isolation in the web of the learner's thinking and feeling. Our book is aimed at word level rather than at sentence level. Each word is a world: we ask the student to explore this world.

Section A
Pre-text activities

Most textbook writers do not focus on words as things-in-themselves but as vehicles of pattern and structure. For the learner, if not always for the teacher, words are exciting. Even lists, uninhibitedly approached, can open up unexpected vistas . . .

A/1 What's in the text?

LEVEL

Elementary to Advanced

TIME

20–30 minutes

PREPARATION

Choose a text and from it select 5–8 items of vocabulary for presentation as a 'word rose' (see below): these should not be 'context-free' (e.g. structure words, neutral or very general adjectives), nor should they be 'key words' that would closely typify the main meaning of the text: the aim should be to allow the students a reasonable chance of coming close to the text without restricting their imaginations.

IN CLASS

1 Put up the word rose on the blackboard.

2 Tell the students that they are going to read a text in which these words appear (not necessarily in the order presented).

3 Ask them, in groups of four, to speculate on the content of the text.

4 Give out copies of the text for comparison and discussion.

VARIATION

Follow (1)–(2) as above, then ask the class to shout out any words suggested by the words you have written up. When you hear words that are in the text, add them to the words already on the blackboard. When you have written, say, twenty more words on the board, carry on with (3) and (4) above.

EXAMPLE

An example of a word rose (based on the text below):

challenge

cattle   digits

wisdom   determine

category

SAMPLE TEXT

How Archimedes' number came up

In the third century BC, the famous Greek mathematician Archimedes issued a challenge to the Alexandrian mathematicians, headed by Eratosthenes. Written in the form of an epigram, Archimedes' challenge begins thus: 'Compute, O friend, the number of oxen of the Sun, giving thy mind thereto, if thou hast a share of wisdom.'

He then goes on to describe, in wonderfully poetic language, a certain herd of cattle, consisting of four types, with bulls and cows of each type. The number of cattle in each of the eight categories is not given, but these numbers are related by nine simple conditions which Archimedes spells out. For example, one of these conditions is that the number of white bulls is equal to the number of yellow bulls plus five-sixths of the number of black bulls. The problem is to determine the number of cattle of each category, and thence the size of the herd.

(Actually, what is required is the smallest possible number, since the nine conditions do not imply a unique answer.)

In his epigram, Archimedes goes on to say that anyone who solves the problem would be 'not unknowing nor unskilled in numbers, but still not yet to be numbered among the wise'. Nothing could be more apt, since there was to elapse 2,000 years before a computer finally found the solution. Clearly Archimedes had a mischievous streak in addition to his principles, and was trying to pull a fast one on his Alexandrian rivals.

In 1880, a German mathematician called Amthor showed that the total number of cattle in Archimedes' herd had to be a number with 206,545 digits, beginning with 7,766. Not surprisingly, Amthor gave up at that point. Over the next 85 years, a further 40 digits were worked out. But it was not until 1965 that mathematicians at the University of Waterloo in Canada finally found the complete solution. It took over seven and a half hours of computation on an IBM 7040 computer. After which no one thought to obtain a printout of the answer! The world had to wait until the problem was solved a second time, using a CRAY-1 computer in 1981, for a published printout. It took the CRAY-1 just ten minutes to crack it. But after 2,000 years, I think Archimedes has to have the last laugh.

(Keith Devlin, *The Guardian*, 21 June 1984)

A/2 Predicting meanings

LEVEL

Elementary to Advanced

TIME

10–20 minutes

PREPARATION

Choose a text and select from it 8–10 words that you think will not be familiar to your students.

IN CLASS

1 Put up the unfamiliar words on the blackboard.

2 Tell the class that you have selected the words from a text that they are about to read, and give them a brief outline of its content.

3 Ask them to take a sheet of paper and rule it into two columns.

4 Ask them to write down each of the words on the blackboard in the left-hand column and then in the right-hand column to write three or four other words that are suggested by it. Tell them that the words they write can be suggested by sound, spelling, possible meaning, or in any other way.

5 Ask the students, in groups of three or four, to compare what they have written.

6 Give out the text.

SAMPLE TEXT   **Magweta**

After World War II, Magweta finds itself with a small foreign exchange surplus and rudimentary armed forces and police force. The country's economy is based on agriculture, predominantly small farms run by one family, but also including a few large estates primarily producing cash crops for export. A civilian political grouping has recently come to power with a policy of rapid industrial development, basing its appeal on nationalistic sentiment amongst the people.

To transform the country, the ruling group starts to import large quantities of machinery, including small amounts of arms, although the cost of the latter is reduced by a grant of military aid from a Western power. Many of the ruling group have been educated in the West and have acquired a Western lifestyle; they set the pace by purchasing cars, radios, and similar luxuries which others in the higher echelons then seek to acquire. The politicians make patriotic speeches which justify the expansion and re-equipping of the military.

After a few years the foreign exchange position has seriously deteriorated and a loan is obtained from the IMF. Exports are encouraged and a major effort is made to expand the production of cash crops through the use of improved agricultural techniques. Selective restrictions are placed on imports in order to stimulate local production, but arms imports continue to increase.

Although there is a short-term improvement helped by some direct foreign investment, a steady decline in the price of cash crop exports, relative to manufactured imports, results in a second application for a loan. This is granted, on condition that the currency is devalued and import restrictions removed. This the government reluctantly accedes to.

The result of this policy is the destruction of embryonic local industry as large foreign concerns, relying heavily on advertising and the lure of Western image, flood the market. Several large tracts of land, some of which were previously farmed under the traditional system, are bought up by a few individuals and firms and converted to produce more crops for export. Employment in traditional agriculture stagnates, and the most vigorous young people leave the land to move into the urban areas, where most of the wealth is concentrated. Rural society declines and shanty towns grow in the shadow of the westernized cities.

(*Bombs for Breakfast*, Campaign Against the Arms Trade, 1981)

A/3 Predicting words

LEVEL

Intermediate to Advanced

TIME

20-25 minutes

PREPARATION

Choose a text with a fairly narrow and predictable set of vocabulary, by virtue of its content and/or style. Examples of suitable texts might be:

– advertisements
– passages from coursebooks (this is an excellent way of stimulating interest in a dull text)
– news items with a well-known theme (arms talks, earthquakes, sports reports)
– fairy stories and folk tales known to the students (e.g. Cinderella, George Washington and the cherry tree, Nasreddin stories)
– instructions, recipes, product descriptions
– popular songs

IN CLASS

1 Tell the students that later in the lesson they will be reading a text/listening to a tape/hearing a story. Give them a very rough idea of what the piece will be about: e.g. in the examples below, tell them they are going to read a short newspaper item about gang-land killings involving ice-cream salesmen in Glasgow/hear an American cowboy song about whisky.

2 Ask the students, in pairs, to predict some of the vocabulary they might encounter in the text. Tell them to produce a list of 8–10 items. Allow dictionaries, and give assistance when asked.

3 Ask the students to form larger groups (8–12) and explain their lists to one another.

4 Give out the texts/play the recording/tell the story.

VARIATION

A Polish colleague, Malgorzata Szwaj, suggests putting up the first part of the title of the piece, and then asking the class to suggest ways of completing it, and to explain what their suggested titles might refer to.

SAMPLE TEXTS

Great Glasgow ice-cream war

A vicious ice-cream vendetta, which has raged for almost two years, may have led to one of Scotland's worst mass-murder cases in many decades.

Six members of the Doyle family died after their Glasgow home was set alight almost two weeks ago. Of the nine people sleeping in the four-storey tenement, only three survived.

Last week it emerged that one of the dead, 18-year-old Andrew Doyle, had been working as a part-time ice-cream seller and had twice been attacked and threatened.

A source within the huge West of Scotland ice-cream business said he believed the murders were a direct result of a final warning—'a frightener that backfired and went badly wrong'.

Ice-cream van sales in the Glasgow area are a highly lucrative business. Most ply their trade on the sprawling council estates where there are few shops. As well as selling ice-cream, most make a healthy living acting as travelling shops.

Rivalry between van drivers and companies is intense and, while respectable firms have generally carved out their own areas, 'cowboys' have moved in, threatening drivers in an attempt to take over their patch.

Andrew Doyle was attacked while in his van and two shotgun blasts fired through his windscreen. Shortly before the fire at his home in Bankhead Street, he was beaten up outside by four men.

Mr Archie McDougall, company secretary of Marchetti Bros, which employed Doyle, said he had been told by the police not to say anything.

But a senior member of one of the larger companies said: 'Over the last two years we have had drivers literally chucking the job on the spot. They have been threatened, their windows smashed, they have been attacked and shotguns pointed at them. We are talking about gangsters with weapons who also deal in drugs and pirate video tapes. In this case, we reckon it was a frightener that backfired.'

The police investigating the murder are reluctant to discuss their inquiries except to say that the ice-cream vendetta is one of their lines of inquiry. Detective Chief Superintendent Charles Craig, who is leading the hunt, said: 'There are several lines of inquiry. The ice-cream vendetta, so called, is one of them.'

(*The Observer*, 29 April 1984)

Rye whisky

I'll eat when I'm hungry,
　I'll drink when I'm dry;
If the hard times don't kill me,
　I'll lay down and die.

Beefsteak when I'm hungry,
　Red liquor when I'm dry,
Greenbacks when I'm hard up,
　And religion when I die.

They say I drink whisky,
　My money's my own;
All them that don't like me
　Can leave me alone.

Sometimes I drink whisky,
　Sometimes I drink rum;
Sometimes I drink brandy,
　At other times none.

Jack o' diamonds, Jack o' diamonds,
　I know you of old.
You've robbed my poor pockets
　Of silver and gold.

Oh, whisky, you villain
　You've been my downfall.
You've kicked me, you've hurt me—
　But I love you for all.

Rye whisky, rye whisky,
　Rye whisky, I cry.
If you don't give me rye whisky,
　I surely will die.

(Traditional US cowboy song)

A/4 Meaning graphs

LEVEL

Elementary to Advanced

TIME

20–30 minutes

PREPARATION

From the text that you wish to work from, choose words that could easily occur in more than one distinct context. Before giving out copies of the text, put up the words you have chosen on the blackboard, numbering them as shown in the examples below.

IN CLASS

1 On the blackboard, draw the two axes of a graph (see below) and give each axis a context or field label, as shown. Ask the students to copy the graph and then, working individually, to place the words in the list (or their numbers) on the graph according to how they associate them with the two fields labelled.

2 Pair the students off and get them to compare their word graphs.

3 Give out copies of the passage and ask them to judge how the words are used there.

EXAMPLES

Graph and word-list for the elementary text '*Leaving home*'.

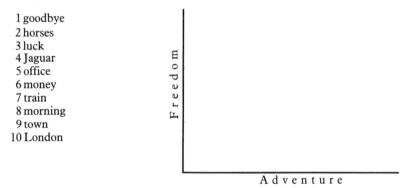

1 goodbye
2 horses
3 luck
4 Jaguar
5 office
6 money
7 train
8 morning
9 town
10 London

Graph and word-list for the upper-intermediate text '*The family situation*', as completed by one student:

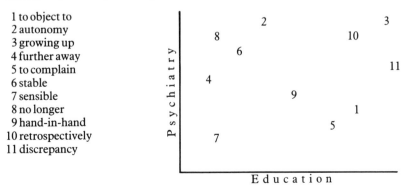

1 to object to
2 autonomy
3 growing up
4 further away
5 to complain
6 stable
7 sensible
8 no longer
9 hand-in-hand
10 retrospectively
11 discrepancy

SAMPLE TEXTS   ## Leaving home

One morning I left home early. I did not say goodbye to my parents.

My father wanted me to work in an office. But I loved horses and I wanted to ride horses. I wanted to be a jockey, but my father didn't understand. So I left home. I was on my own.

I took a bus from the centre of town and then I walked. Soon I reached the motorway. I wanted to get to London, but I didn't have enough money for a train. I was hoping to get a lift in a car. Every time a car came, I put out my hand. But the cars didn't stop. Half an hour passed. And then my luck changed.

A big red Jaguar came up behind me. I saw the driver look at me. Then the car slowed down and stopped.

The family situation

Mr and Mrs Abbott appear quiet, ordinary people. When Maya was eighteen Mrs Abbott was described by a psychiatric social worker as 'a most agreeable woman, who appeared to be very friendly and easy to live with'. Mr Abbott has 'a quiet manner but a kindly one'. He seemed 'a very sensible man, but less practical than his wife'. There did not appear to be much that he would not do for his family. He had excellent health, and impressed the interviewer as 'a very stable personality'.

Maya was born when her mother was twenty and her father thirty. When his daughter was born, Mr Abbott had been reading of an excavation of a Mayan tomb. 'Just the name for my little girl,' he thought.

Mother and father agreed that until sent away from home at eight, Maya had been her Daddy's girl. She would wake him early in the morning and they would go swimming. She was always hand-in-hand with him. They sat close together at table, and he was the one to say prayers with her last thing at night. They frequently went for long walks together.

Apart from brief visits home, Maya lived away from her parents from eight until the age of fourteen. When she came home to live permanently with them, they complained she was changed. She was no longer their little girl. She wanted to study. She did not want to go swimming, or to go for long walks with her father any more. She no longer wanted to pray with him. She wanted to read the Bible herself, by herself. She objected to her father expressing his affection for her by sitting close to her at meals. She wanted to sit further away from him. Nor did she want to go to the cinema with her mother. In the house, she wanted to handle things and to do things for herself, such as (mother's example) washing a mirror without first telling her mother.

These changes in Maya, mentioned by her parents retrospectively as the first signs of illness, seem to us to be ordinary expressions of growing up. What is of interest is the discrepancy between her parents' judgement of these developments and ours.

(R. D. Laing and A. Esterson, *Sanity and Madness in the Family*, Penguin Books)

A/5 Criminal records

LEVEL

Elementary to Advanced

TIME

30–40 minutes

PREPARATION

Choose the key words from a text.

IN CLASS

1 Write up on the blackboard a skeleton 'criminal record card' of the type shown below (column 1 only).

2 Fill in a sample 'criminal record' as in column 2.

3 Point out that words could also be said to have criminal records, and give a fairly concrete example in column 3:

1	2	3
Name	John Smith	*fat*
Place of residence	3 Packer Street West Croydon	*body*
Known associates	Peter Jackson Arthur Baines	*carbohydrates cholesterol*
Criminal record	robbery, terrorism, kidnapping	*heart disease ugliness*

4 Write up on the blackboard a list of words from the text you have chosen. For the intermediate text overleaf this could be:

land	*value*
belong	*rent*
market	*commodity*

Ask the students to make out 'criminal record cards' for each of the words you have written up.

5 Ask the students to form small groups (3–5) and tell each other what they have written and why.

6 Ask the class to read the text.

EXAMPLE

In one group, students produced the following:

Name	*value*	*commodity*	*rent*
Place of residence	*jewellery safe*	*shop*	*Cambridge*
Known associates	*money investment*	*sell buy*	*landlady*
Criminal record	*stealing cheating*	*greed*	*dirty room bad food*

SAMPLE TEXT **Land**

To us in Africa land was always recognized as belonging to the community. Each individual within our society had a right to the use of the land, because otherwise he could not earn his living and one cannot have the right to life without also having the right to some means of sustaining life. But the African's right to land was simply the right to use it; he had no other right to it, nor did it occur to him to try and claim one. The foreigner introduced a completely different concept—the concept of land as a marketable commodity. According to this system, a person could claim a piece of land as his own private property whether he intended to use it or not. I could take a few square miles of land, call them 'mine', and then go off to the moon. All I had to do to gain a living from 'my' land was to charge a rent to the people who wanted to use it. If this piece of land was in an urban area I had no need to develop it at all; I could leave it to the fools who were prepared to develop all the other pieces of land surrounding 'my' piece, and in doing so automatically to raise the market value of mine. Then I could come down from the moon and demand that these fools pay me through their noses for the high value of 'my' land—a value which they themselves had created for me while I was enjoying myself on the moon! Such a system is not only foreign to us, it is completely wrong.

(Julius K. Nyerere, *Ujamaa*, Oxford University Press 1968)

A/6 Ungrammatical gender

Many teachers might be horrified at the idea of *encouraging* students to associate English words with gender—it's hard enough to stop Gaston saying 'When I picked up the cup, she broke'. But quite apart from the grammar, many words are, for some of us at least, gender-loaded . . .

LEVEL   **Intermediate to Advanced**

TIME   **30–40 minutes**

PREPARATION   Choose a text and list 10–12 words and phrases in it that the class are likely to find hard. In the following example text these could be:

bite the dust   offensive   crop   counter-attack   on his side
bumper   handling   contain   incursion   dumping
curb   tirade

IN CLASS   1 Put up your list on the blackboard and ask the students to check (with dictionaries, from each other, or by asking you) that they understand all the words.

2 Ask the students, working individually, to divide the words into male and female. Tell them that this has nothing to do with ideas of

grammatical gender or 'dictionary meaning', but should express their own *feelings* about the words.

3 Invite the students to discuss in pairs why they sexed the words as they did.

4 Give out the text for the class to read.

EXAMPLE

Here is what one student produced:

Male	Female
bite the dust	*crop*
offensive	*on his side*
counter-attack	*handling*
bumper	*contain*
incursion	*tirade*
dumping	
curb	

SAMPLE TEXT

Redskins bite the dust in tomato war

The winter offensive in The Great Mexican–American Tomato War opens this week in southern Arizona. Truckloads of gleaming, ripe Mexican tomatoes will roll north across the border, bound for American salad bowls. At the same time, American tomato growers in Florida, where the climate allows them to produce a winter crop, will launch a counter-attack with their secret weapon, a tomato code-named MH-1.

A rugged little fighter, the MH-1 seems the kind of tomato anyone would want to have on his side. It is so sturdy that its skin can survive a fall at 13.4 miles an hour—or more than two and a half times the force that American car bumpers must withstand in a crash.

The MH-1 was raised in Florida to be picked by machines more cheaply than Mexican tomatoes can be picked by hand. Hence its name: MH stands for 'mechanical handling'.

The Florida growers hoped that, armed with the MH-1, they would be able to defeat, or at least contain, the Mexican incursion. But they were wrong. The Mexicans kept coming with cheaper tomatoes— and this year things look worse than ever.

The Florida growers are convinced that the Mexicans are dumping tomatoes on the US at prices below production cost in a deliberate effort to drive them out of business. So they have demanded that the US government curb the imports.

Unfortunately for the Florida growers, the climate is not ripe for such demands. The US is engaged in delicate negotiations to buy oil and natural gas from Mexico. And, as one government source said, 'You don't throw tomatoes at somebody who may be able to solve your energy crisis.'

Then there is the even more delicate question of the difference in taste between a Mexican tomato, ripened on the plant, and the MH-1. One Democratic Congressman, Henry Reuss from Wisconsin, was so inflamed by what he called the 'cotton-wool' taste of the Florida

tomatoes that he wrote a long tirade about it in the *New York Times*.
Reuss noted that in order to cut costs, the Florida growers machine-
harvest their tomatoes only three times a year, instead of picking the
ripe ones every day, as the Mexicans do.

(*The Sunday Times*, January 1980)

A/7 Look, remember, and complete the set

LEVEL   **Elementary to Advanced**

TIME   **30–40 minutes**

PREPARATION   From a narrative or descriptive text which you wish the class to read,
select 25–30 of those vocabulary items which for you best reflect the
mood and action of the passage. Set out the words you have chosen as a
word jumble like this one, which is taken from the text following, and
prepare sufficient copies for each person in the group.

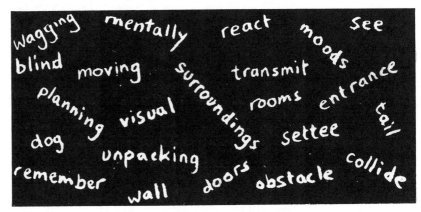

IN CLASS   1 Give out the word jumbles face-down to each member of the group.

2 Tell the class that they will have 15 seconds (or more if you have
chosen a long list) to look at the jumbles, then tell them to turn over
their sheets and read.

3 When the time limit is up, tell the class to turn the jumbles face-
down again. Then ask them, working individually, to write out all the
words they can remember.

4 Then ask them to write down any more words they think might fit
the scene or action suggested by the words they have remembered.
They might like to use a different coloured pen for this.

5 Ask the students to discuss in pairs the words they have written
down, and the text that they imagine contains them.

6 Give out copies of the text.

Acknowledgement
This idea was suggested by a picture recall exercise presented by Alan Maley at a conference of the International Association of Teachers of English as a Foreign Language (IATEFL) in December 1979.

SAMPLE TEXT

Moving house

It took the upheaval of moving house to bring home to me again that I could not see. This may sound odd. But having Emma, I could see: not in a visual sense, obviously, but I knew what was going on around me as she reacted to her surroundings. All her feelings and moods transmitted themselves through the harness. I could always tell if there was an obstacle ahead because of the way she slowed up and hesitated ever so slightly. I knew when we were passing another dog, because I could feel her looking, and her tail wagging.

But around the house it was different. Moving in a room, or from one room to another, a blind person is always mentally planning. And moving to a new house, you have to start all over again. Don helped me move in, and we had a hectic time: he put up curtain rails and changed electric plugs, while I carried on the endless business of unpacking. Emma and I collapsed into bed at about two in the morning. In next to no time, it seemed, I heard someone knocking outside (it was, in fact, Don) and I quickly got out of bed. Then I realized I could not remember exactly where the door was. I felt I was in a fitted wardrobe. After trying another wall, and coming back again to the fitted wardrobe, I finally found the right door. Pausing only to collide with the settee that I had forgotten had been put in the middle of the living room, I got to the front door. There was no one there. Then I remembered there was a back door as well, where Don was patiently waiting. It took me a long time to become accustomed to all the different doors, after being used to my flat with its one entrance and fewer rooms.

(Sheila Hocken, *Emma and I*, Gollancz 1977)

A/8 Words on a map

Word associations are complex and powerful. In this exercise, students are invited to explore the personal connections that words may have *before* they meet them in a text. As with many exercises of this type, such a 'focus' activity may prove more powerful than the text itself. Where teachers are forced to use dull prescribed material, this may be an advantage. With more compelling texts, caution should be observed.

LEVEL	**Intermediate to Advanced**
TIME	**20–30 minutes**
PREPARATION	Choose a passage and pick out 10–12 words and phrases from it to focus on. For the passage given below, we suggest these:

variations	*to run into*
component	*mobility*
to generate	*daring to change*
experiment	*justifications*
in one's own voice	*standard rules*

Choose an image (a map of a well-known country, picture of a well-known person, a symbol) and be ready to show it to the students, e.g.

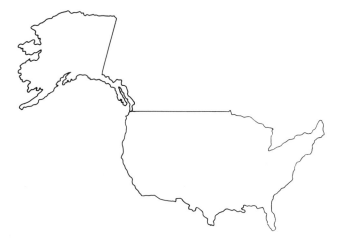

IN CLASS

1 Show the image to the class and give them the list of words. Ask them to decide individually which words apply in some way to the image. Alternatively, give out copies of the image and ask them to write the words on it in appropriate positions.

2 Ask them to compare notes with their neighbours.

3 Give out copies of the text.

SAMPLE TEXT

Children at play

Watching children play, I decided that if one presents young children with the components of games, they will generate games themselves. Children experiment with different ways of doing things, whereas adults get accustomed to believing there is one right and one wrong way to do things. Creating a game is much like discovering how to write in one's own voice. Making games, writing, building are all ways young people can discover that they can put things into the world, that they can have some control over life.

The other day I ran into some children who were playing their own version of chess. The knights jumped two squares at a time, since they galloped like horses. The queen, rooks, pawns and bishops moved in their regular ways, though the king was given the mobility of a queen. When I came upon the game a young student was telling the kids how wrong they were in daring to change the rules of the game, that they would never be 'real' chess players if they didn't play the rules. One of the kids said she didn't want to be a real chess player but was curious about what happened when you changed the rules. The new game was interesting but the student teacher insisted it wasn't a game and forced the kids to play by the standard rules. When I mentioned to him that there were dozens of variations of chess played throughout the world, he claimed that the only justification for letting children play games in school was to accustom them to learning to play by the rules. I disagree.

(H. R. Kohl, *Writing, Maths and Games*, Methuen 1977)

A/9 Cards on the table

This exercise is particularly useful in clarifying people's ideas about a topic or attitude before reading a text that will be used as the basis for discussion or essay-writing.

LEVEL **Intermediate to Advanced**

TIME **20–30 minutes**

PREPARATION 1 For the first class: prepare a set of 24 cards, each bearing a different word. Choose the words from a fairly well-defined area of human concern, e.g.

Things and ideas close to the individual:

man	animal	enemy	boy	mind	father	child	pet
son	soul	family	baby	friend	heart	daughter	mother
god	stomach	group	head	woman	girl	adult	blood

Social concerns and ideas:

home	school	neighbourhood	nest	friends	garden	house	language
nation	estate	conversation	property	land	flat	society	country
speech	hospital	institution	belongings	family	wife	cottage	locality

2 For later classes: choose a passage, preferably one expressing a strong theme or point of view, and pick out 24 words and/or phrases from it which typify its content. Prepare a set of 24 cards, each bearing a different word or phrase, for every 6–8 students in the class. From the text below, we have selected these:

threat	school	psychiatrist	police	nursed	neighbour	home	perpetrated
suicide	ill	teenager	mother	statistics	social services	hospital	mentally
shop	theft	refuge	magistrate	community	accused	vandalism	anorexia nervosa

IN THE FIRST CLASS

1 Arrange the classroom so that the group(s) of students can stand round a table or tables.

2 Lay out a set of cards face-up in random order on the table(s).

3 Ask the group(s) to arrange the cards in groups of three (or four, or six) according to meaning. Stress that (a) the group must agree unanimously and (b) all the cards must be used.

4 Invite the group(s) to justify their card arrangement. If there is more than one group, get them to circulate and see what other groups have done.

IN LATER CLASSES

Follow the same procedure as above, but use cards bearing words derived from a text. The students may read the text before working on the cards, afterwards, or both. The exercise can thus be used as a lead-in to a text and/or as a way of passing comment on it and stimulating criticism and discussion.

SAMPLE TEXT

My mother

Above five years before her death my mother ceased her threats of suicide and embarked on a life of persistent theft. It must have been a sweet moment when a shop assistant I had once fined in the magistrate's court for shoplifting asked: 'What are you going to do about your mother's shoplifting?'

The local shops frisked my mother's pockets and shopping bag, but never bargained for the capacity of directoire knickers with strong elastics. So she still got away with a great deal, although once she shed onions and carrots as she walked.

'You mustn't do that sort of thing,' said the psychiatrist, now being chased up by the police and the social services. She was now in deep depression at being accused of stealing, and he took her into hospital for a course of electro-convulsive therapy. It lifted the depression and she was quite a happy shoplifter, and the only place she was safe in was the bank.

Next came illegal entry. She would go into houses and take anything portable. During the hours of darkness my mother, then 83, fell over a wall between two houses, suffered appalling lacerations, and left a trail of blood back to her home.

'Now they will be obliged to take her in!' said the GP. With a suitcase in the boot I drove her to the clinic.

'You have made a mess of yourself,' said the psychiatrist. I drove her home—my home— and nursed her for six weeks.

With great resilience she became as active as ever, and the community was beset by teenage vandalism. The police visited schools, and my mother's neighbour, after several bouts of damage, bought a huge Alsatian, which, he assured me, would tear to pieces anyone who touched the car.

Watchers, some time after that, witnessed the car vandalism. My mother selected the car, went into the house for an instrument, and perpetrated the damage. A frustrated policeman told me: 'And to cap it all, the ruddy dog was helping her!'

'This time she will be taken in,' said both GP and social workers, but she was not. Her last refuge was anorexia nervosa.

'It is time you had some relief,' the psychiatrist told me. He proposed taking her into the psycho-geriatric ward for three weeks.

Before that time came she had another fall. Lacerated and shocked, she was taken into the local general hospital. The following morning I was told by the ward sister that she was much improved, and eating her breakfast as if she had not seen food for a month. A few minutes later she rang back. My mother had choked to death. She had joined the statistics of those mentally ill who are successfully maintained within the community.

(Clarice Maizel, *The Guardian*, 19 December 1983)

Section B
Working with texts

B/1 Customizing a text

LEVEL   Intermediate to Advanced

TIME   20–30 minutes

PREPARATION   From the reading passage you propose to use next with your class, select a dozen or so words to focus on. Write these down. Then prepare a sheet of thirty to forty different words (not only synonyms) from which alternatives to those in the text can be chosen. (See the example on the next page.)

IN CLASS   1 Give the students the reading passage to look through.

2 Slowly say the words you have chosen, while the students underline them in the passage.

3 Give out the sheet of alternative words.

4 Ask the students to select substitutes from the sheet for the words underlined.

5 In pairs the students look at and discuss each other's choices.

Acknowledgement
This is derived from an idea proposed by Gail Moraro, an Adult Migrant Education teacher in Melbourne, in *ESL Teachers' Exchange*, December 1983.

SAMPLE TEXT   **Air bases**

The eight main airbases are the most prominent aspect of American forces in Britain. Unlike the many US communications and intelligence facilities, command centres and reserve bases here, the giant airbases are well known to many members of the public. Despite making bullseye targets for any attacker, however, these forces do not contribute in any direct way to British air defences. On the contrary, they impose a substantial additional burden on Royal Air Force defence fighters, which are already stretched in defending their own airbases and have not been regarded, for 25 years, as capable of protecting British cities from air attack.

Britain asks no rent for US use of British bases. Construction costs of runways and new facilities are shared between NATO, including Britain, and the United States. Building costs are allocated according to the purpose of each base. If a unit is allocated to NATO, the common NATO funds will pay for many facilities to be built to an agreed standard, including runways and shelters. Exceptionally, if new facilities are for bilateral UK–US use, then costs will be split directly between the two countries. The US has to pay entirely for the many British-based units which are operated for the unilateral purposes of the United States, and not committed to NATO. Most of the building work is supervised by the Department of the Environment, and costs are reimbursed by the US government.

Although operating costs are normally all paid by the Pentagon, some tasks—such as air defence missile units around the main bases, or guarding cruise missile convoys—are the financial responsibility of the RAF.

(Duncan Campbell, *The Unsinkable Aircraft Carrier*, Michael Joseph 1984)

Words for dictation:

prominent	*facilities*	*command*	*public*	*target*
burden	*stretched*	*attack*	*runway*	*shelters*
operated	*unilateral*	*supervised*	*tasks*	*missile*

Alternative words:

exciting	*election*	*confused*	*espionage*	*extended*
run	*alarming*	*threat*	*designed*	*one-sided*
payment	*tarmac*	*bomb*	*services*	*advice*
expensive	*tax*	*money*	*private*	*dictate* *labour*
collection	*party*	*control*	*relation*	*demand* *army*
subvert	*side*	*manager*	*regime*	*dominate*
communist	*oppose*	*forces*	*population*	*thought*
surprise	*hideouts*	*superb*		

B/2 Where else do they fit?

LEVEL

Intermediate to Advanced

TIME

30–45 minutes

PREPARATION

Choose a passage and list 8–12 words from it that can be contextualized in other fields. Here are words from the sample text overleaf:

suit

ball   *hitch*

rough   *space*

gear   *reckon*

automatically

Then prepare three-word sets of other words to indicate particular fields in which the words from your text may be recontextualized. For our example you might produce:

(suit) : fit   (ball) : party   (space) : typewriter
         belong   reception   comma
         blend   dance   misprint

          (gear) : brake   (rough) : smooth
                   carburettor   sticky
                   clutch   slippery

(hitch) : snag   (reckon) : believe   (automatically) : machine
          delay   fact   operate
          problem   opinion   process

IN CLASS

1 Tell the students to read the sample passage below and check the words they don't know.

2 Give them the words you have selected from the passage.

3 Give out or put up on the blackboard the three-word sets you have constructed and ask the students to fit as many of the text words as they can into the sets. They should be asked to work individually.

4 Ask the students, in groups of 3–5, to compare their matchings. As some words may fit more than one set, this is likely to produce a certain amount of disagreement and discussion.

SAMPLE TEXT

The towel

A towel has immense psychological value. For some reason, if a *strag* (strag: non-hitch hiker) discovers that a hitch hiker has his towel with him, he will automatically assume that he is also in possession of a toothbrush, face flannel, soap, tin of biscuits, flask, compass, map, ball of string, gnat spray, wet weather gear, space suit, etc., etc. Furthermore, the strag will then happily lend the hitch hiker any of these or a dozen other items that the hitch hiker might accidentally have 'lost'. What the strag will think is that any man who can hitch the length and breadth of the galaxy, rough it, slum it, struggle against terrible odds, win through, and still know where his towel is is clearly a man to be reckoned with.

(Douglas Adams, *Hitch Hiker's Guide to the Galaxy*, Pan 1979)

B/3 Correct the teacher

LEVEL

Elementary to Advanced

TIME

25–35 minutes in the first class and **45–60 minutes** in the second

PREPARATION

Write out an anecdote in short sentences. Pick 10–15 words from it that you want the students to focus on, and write paraphrases of them. Substitute your paraphrases for the words in the text, then write out the original words on cards to be given out to the class. You will need one card for each student, so if you have picked out ten words and your class is thirty strong, put each word on three cards. Here is an example anecdote incorporating paraphrases:

SAMPLE TEXT

He was a hefty man in his mid-fifties. He had a large *stomach* which looked just right behind the wheel of his thirty-ton *lorry*.

One day, driving along a *bendy* country road, he saw a bridge over the road ahead of him. 'Maximum height: 14ft' he read on the *notice*.

He *stopped* and *got out*. He looked from his lorry to the bridge, scratching his head *thoughtfully*.

'My lorry's 14 feet 1 inch,' he thought to himself. 'It'll never get through there.'

Just at that moment a motor-bike *policeman* roared up and asked what the *problem* was.

'Can't get through,' the trucker told him.

'Easy,' said the other. 'Just let your tyres down an inch or two and have them *re-inflated* on the other side.'

The driver thought about this *attentively* for several minutes. 'No use,' he said *weightily*. 'It's at the top it won't get through, not at the bottom.'

The original words are put on cards for the students:

Paraphrases in text	Original words on cards
stomach	*paunch*
lorry	*truck*
bendy	*twisting*
notice	*sign*
stopped	*pulled up*
got out	*climbed down*
thoughtfully	*pensively*
policeman	*cop*
problem	*trouble*
re-inflated	*pumped up again*
attentively	*carefully*
weightily	*ponderously*

IN CLASS

1 Read the story once through so that the students get the outline of it.

2 Give out the cards to the students. Give them a chance to check that they know the meaning of the words on them.

3 Tell the class that you are going to read the story again, but that this time they should stop you as soon as they hear a paraphrase of a word they have on their cards. After stopping you, they are to repeat your sentence, substituting the word.

4 Read through the story again.

IN THE SECOND CLASS

Once your students have done two or three exercises like the one above, ask them to produce anecdotes of their own.

1 Put the students in groups of three and ask each group to write an anecdote of their own.

2 Ask the groups to prepare 6–12 paraphrases of interesting words in their texts and to put these on cards or slips of paper.

3 Ask each group of three to join with another group.

4 Within each pair of groups, ask one member of group **A** to read the group anecdote slowly to the members of group **B**. The cards should then be given out to the members of **B**, and the activity proceeds as in the first class (above).

5 Repeat the activity, using group **B**'s anecdote.

VARIATION

With beginners and very elementary students, give out copies of the text, then simply dictate some words extracted from it: they should underline the words they hear. In a later class, mix in a few paraphrases of words or phrases in the passage.

Acknowledgement
We owe this activity to Lou Spaventa.

B/4 On the walls

This exercise is designed mainly for classes sharing the same mother tongue.

LEVEL

Beginner to Elementary

TIME

15 minutes

PREPARATION

Get together a collection of posters, maps, and other textual realia, and pin it up round the walls of the classroom. Then choose ten or so words contained in the texts on the walls and prepare a list of their translations into the students' mother tongue.

IN CLASS

Put the list of translations on the blackboard. Tell the students that their English equivalents are to be found 'somewhere on the walls', and ask them to look for them.

Acknowledgement
We learnt this technique from Jean Cureau.

B/5 Tape montage

LEVEL **Intermediate to Advanced**

TIME **15 minutes**

PREPARATION Piece together a 3–4 minute tape montage from radio news items, mixed with bits of course tapes, eavesdroppings of a previous class, etc.

IN CLASS 1 Play the tape to the group once only.

2 Ask the group to write down everything they remember, and any comments on topic, programme, etc. that they wish.

3 Ask the students to form groups of 3–4, and to pool their notes and comments.

4 Play the tape again straight through.

5 Ask the groups to produce a one-minute 'broadcast' sketch or dialogue based on their notes: i.e. incorporating vocabulary heard or suggested by the topics.

VARIATIONS 1 Make your montage from fragments of radio broadcasts, interference, music, call-signs, etc. Include short stretches of talk in various languages as well as English and the mother tongue(s), but don't allow any stretch to be longer than ten seconds.

2 To focus more narrowly on particular lexical items, record news items from a variety of sources, and then follow up the exercise with a reading comprehension based on the same stories presented in the newspapers.

B/6 A memory game

LEVEL **Intermediate to Advanced**

TIME **15–25 minutes**

PREPARATION Choose a shortish text, and select from it 8–10 words: include in your list 3–4 words that appear several times, and a couple that are repeated many times (e.g. pronouns, articles). Count the number of times that each item on the list appears in the text. Add to the list 2–3 words that are connected with or are of similar meaning to words in the text, but which do not appear in it. (See example text overleaf.)

IN CLASS 1 Give out the text, and ask the students to read it through once. Give them a fairly ungenerous time limit for this.

2 Remove, or ask them to turn over, the texts.

3 Give out, or put up on the blackboard, the list of words you have prepared, *without* the frequency count.

4 Ask the students, singly or in pairs, to remember or guess the number of times each word appeared in the passage. Tell them that there are a few words on the list that were not in the passage at all. Ask them *not* to refer back to the texts.

5 Put up the frequency count for each word, and ask them to read through the texts again.

SAMPLE TEXT

Wootton Major

There was a village once, not very long ago for those with long memories, nor very far away for those with long legs. Wootton Major it was called because it was larger than Wootton Minor, a few miles away deep in the trees; but it was not very large, though it was at that time prosperous, and a fair number of folk lived in it, good, bad, and mixed, as is usual.

It was a remarkable village in its way, being well known in the country round about for the skill of its workers in various crafts, but most of all for its cooking. It had a large Kitchen which belonged to the Village Council, and the Master Cook was an important person. The Cook's House and the Kitchen adjoined the Great Hall, the largest and oldest building in the place and the most beautiful.

(J. R. R. Tolkien, *Smith of Wootton Major*, Allen and Unwin 1967)

Word list:

village	(2)	*house*	(0)
very	(3)	*most*	(1)
small	(0)	*kitchen*	(2)
long	(3)	*few*	(1)
man	(0)	*people*	(0)

B/7 Two-language texts

This exercise type is designed for classes sharing the same mother tongue, and particularly for those who are aiming at a reading knowledge of English. We have found it an excellent way of getting beginners gradually to assimilate new vocabulary by setting it in a context that has not been denatured, as in so many target-language beginners' readers.

LEVEL

Beginner to Elementary

TIME

15 minutes per session over several class meetings

PREPARATION

Take an English text that your students will find gripping, and translate it into their mother tongue. Leave one word or so per sentence in English: choose words that can be guessed fairly accurately from the sentence context, and words that are repeated in the text.

Pick a fairly long text that the students can work on for a few minutes per session over several weeks. Leave progressively more of the text in English, but do not be tempted to put too much in English too soon, or the reading will become heavy.

For obvious reasons we cannot provide materials for your particular students: instead, see below for a text that assumes you are a beginner in Modern Greek.

IN CLASS

Hand out the day's instalment and then disappear. After the students have worked through several sessions, they may feel a need for discussion in their mother tongue.

SAMPLE TEXT

The Barbarians come in the night . . .

When the telephone *kudunísi* in the middle of the night, something unusual is happening. Just such a *tilefónima* woke me up at dawn on the 21st of April 1967. From the other end *tís gramís* the journalist, George Papachristophilou, told me in a trembling voice:
'There's been a coup—there are tanks everywhere and they're surrounding everything—leave your *spíti!*'
'Are you serious?' I *rótisa* him.
'*Né*, I tell you, I can see rifles, machine-guns, helmets, *stratiótes*, get out while you can!' I put down the *tiléfono* and stayed silent for some seconds. Then I began dialling *arithmús*. All *gramés* to the centre had been cut off.
Some *tiléfona* in the suburbs were still answering. I managed to speak to a very few of my *fílus* and tell them the terrible news.
By now my *yinéka* had woken up. As she got my clothes together she *rotúse* me:
'But who's behind the coup? Is it going to go on a long time? You've only just come back and now you *févgis* again. Thank God you managed to come back home from prison . . . You must *tilefonísis* me after lunch to let me know you're OK. You mustn't *niázese* about us— look after yourself and be careful . . . And let me know how I can *vrísko* you . . .'
Our talking *xípnise* my two daughters, Eva, who was in her second year at primary school, and Iro who still went to *nipiagogío*. They thought they had to go to school earlier. I explained to them that it wasn't yet *óra* and that I was going to have to be away from *spíti* for quite some time.

(T. Dimos, *2340 Meres stin Paranomiá*, Glaros 1977)

Acknowledgements
The idea of using bi-lingual texts in the way described came to us from reading Anthony Burgess's *A Clockwork Orange*. A good, sustained example in German/English is Werner Lansburgh's *Dear Doosie* (Fischer Verlag 1979).

B/8 Hunt the misfits

LEVEL

Intermediate to Advanced

TIME

20–35 minutes

PREPARATION

Choose a short passage that you think will be easy for your students. Change some of the words in it so that it no longer makes proper sense. In class you will need copies of both the original passage and the doctored one. (See example material on the next page.)

IN CLASS

1 Give each of the students a copy of the doctored text and ask them to read it. Don't tell them what you have done to the text—let it dawn on them. Eventually one or more students will point out that there is something wrong, and you can ask them to make corrections.

2 When they have corrected as much as they can, ask them to check each other's work.

3 Give out the undoctored passage.

IN A LATER CLASS

When the students have done two or three editing exercises like the one above, give them an undoctored text and invite them to doctor it: students take even more pleasure in constructing the texts than in 'correcting' them.

Choose for this purpose a text that presents few comprehension problems, and make sure that the students have dictionaries to hand. Above all, the students must know enough to feel that the text is within their grasp (The text 'Viaduct Rescue' on the next page would be appropriate for a fairly advanced group.)

VARIATION

1 Put up the following sentence on the blackboard and invite the class to correct it:

Mario is not holy bad.

2 Now put up this sentence and invite them to introduce a similar, creative mistake:

Peter is my best friend.

3 Ask them, in small groups, to deform other simple sentences, e.g.

London is the capital of England.
Elena asked me to feed the cats.
There's no money in the bank.

SAMPLE TEXTS

CHARLIE CAIROLI THE CLOWN DIES AGED 70

Charlie Cairoli, one of the best known circus clowns to perform in this country, died yesterday at the age of 70. Instantly recognizable with his visual hallmarks of bowler hat and shiny red nose he had delighted audiences at the Blackpool Tower circus for nearly forty years.

Cairoli was born in France, the son of a juggler, and began his performing career at the age of five. He came to Britain in 1938 and became the leading feature of the Blackpool Tower circus, where he remained until ill health forced him to retire last year. He had a great affinity with children.

[*The Times*, 18 February 1980]

CHARLIE CAIROLI THE CLOWN DIES AGED 70

Charlie Cairoli, one of the best known circus clones to perform in this country, died yesterday at the age of 70. Instantly recognizable with his visual hallmarks of bowler hat and polished red nose he had delighted congregations at the Blackpool Tower circus for less than forty years.

Cairoli was born in France, the son of a juggler, and began his deforming career at the age of five. He came to Britain in 1938 and became the leading feature of the Blackpool Tower circus, where he remained until ill health invited him to retire last year. He had a small affinity with children.

VIADUCT RESCUE

An ambulance man was lowered from a motorway viaduct yesterday to reach a lorry driver who survived a 100-foot plunge after his vehicle jack-knifed.

Mr Eddie Maloney, aged 31, volunteered to be lowered by nylon rope from the Thelwall viaduct of the M6 near Warrington, Cheshire, to give first aid and pain-killing gas to the driver, who was still conscious.

Mr Maloney, who made the descent in high winds, said afterwards: 'It was pretty hair-raising. My legs were like jelly when I got to the bottom.'

The driver, Mr Peter Worth, aged 26, of Bolton, was thrown through the cab windscreen when his lorry jack-knifed on the viaduct. He was taken to the intensive care unit of Warrington General Hospital.

[*The Guardian*, 23 February 1980]

B/9 Ghost definitions

LEVEL Elementary to Intermediate

TIME 20 minutes

PREPARATION Choose a text, and underline 8–10 words and phrases in it. Then, at the foot of the page, write definitions of these words, in no particular order, together with definitions of 2–4 other words not in the text. Make one copy for each student in the class. (See example below.)

IN CLASS 1 Explain how you prepared the definitions.

2 Ask the students to match the definitions to the underlined words, and then to find words to suit the remaining definitions.

3 Ask them to look at the work of two or three other students in the class.

SAMPLE TEXT **Crossing Morecambe Bay**

There is no *route* or path which can be taken *regularly*, in safety, over the sands of Morecambe Bay. In November 1963, sixteen Royal Marines on a *route march* from Hest Bank to Barrow-in-Furness nearly got themselves into serious trouble before I rushed out and put them back on to a safe course. They had started out one hour before I had suggested, and so were *heading* straight for deep water. Then there was a *lad* who tried to cross the bay on a bicycle, but soon found how hopeless it was when he had to be rescued *in mid-channel*. Changes are so *diverse* and so frequent. Each tide *shifts* the sand in one direction or another, and along the coast, quite large *chunks* of rock can be moved great distances. Even to someone with experience, such conditions are not always easily *predicted*.

(Cedric Robinson, *Sand Pilot of Morecambe Bay*, David and Charles 1980)

a young man	*half-way across the water*
often	*of different kinds*
thick, solid lumps	*kept away from*
way taken from one place	*moving in a particular direction*
to another	*changes the position of*
natural stream of water	*at evenly-spaced intervals*
long journey on foot made	*known in advance*
by soldiers in training	

B/10 Please do not read this notice!

Many teachers urge students 'Don't worry about the words you don't know—just aim at getting the gist.' One way of doing this is to get them to cross out all the words and expressions they don't know, and to try to make sense of what is left of the text. Human nature being what it is, however, it is often precisely the crossed-out words that are learnt and remembered . . .

LEVEL	**Elementary to Advanced**
TIME	**20–40 minutes**

PREPARATION

Choose a text that is a little harder than the students are accustomed to reading. (An example for upper-intermediate students will be found below.) Make copies. Make sure your students have a supply of coloured pencils or ballpoints.

IN CLASS

1 Give out the copies of the text.

2 Ask them to look through the text, and to cross out any words or phrases that are unfamiliar, or are being used in an unfamiliar way. To do this, they should use a colour-coded scheme, e.g.

    black: words I don't know
    green: words I recognize, but still don't understand
    red: words my teacher probably didn't know yesterday

3 Ask the students, in groups of 2–4, to compare their crossed-out words.

SAMPLE TEXT

What is a word?

The first impression of a literate language user is that the notion of *word* is basic and simple. A word is whatever appears between blanks and punctuation marks on a page. Even in spoken language, it seems quite reasonable to attempt to say something 'one word at a time'. As with many features of language, though, a simple definition works for a great majority of the items in the language but also leaves many unsolved problems.

    Structural linguists emphasized the need to provide clear formal definitions of the components of linguistic utterances, and in doing this found the need to talk about a unit called a *morpheme*, which corresponded in some but not all ways to our common-sense notion of a word. The morpheme is defined to be the basic unit of meaning, and several morphemes can be combined in a single word. New solutions come up in trying to formalize the idea of 'unit of meaning', but to a large extent we can get agreement on the presence of morphemes. The word *computerization* is made up of *compute, -er, -ize,* and *-ation*. In German, the phrase *life insurance company employee* is expressed as the single multi-morpheme word *Lebensversicherungsgesellschaftsangestell-ter*. Some languages (called *agglutinating languages*) build up complex words to convey some of the same information that we express with syntactic structures in English. In Turkish, for example, much of the verb and preposition structure is 'glued together'.

In view of phenomena like these, it is clear that our notion of what constitutes a single word cannot depend on our intuitions about how much separate meaning each word should convey. It is also not reliable to depend on the way things are spelled or pronounced. Even in English, which compared to many languages has a clear separation of words, there are examples that cause problems for analysis. The phrases *can not*, *cannot*, and *can't* share a common meaning. *Can not* is clearly two words, but the others are less certain. The term *contraction* is used for a class of problematic structures such as *we've*, *wouldn't* and *she'll*, which behave very much like single words although they are derived from pairs of words.

(Terry Winograd, *Language as a Cognitive Process*, Addison-Wesley 1983)

B/11 Scrambled lines

LEVEL	**Elementary to Advanced**
TIME	**15–30 minutes**
PREPARATION	Choose a short paragraph from a newspaper. Cut up the text line by line and rearrange it, before making copies for the class. Alternatively, re-type the text, rearranging the sequence of lines, but preserving each line intact, as in the three scrambled examples.
IN CLASS	1 Give out copies of the scrambled text to the group. Ask the students to read through the text and to ask you or each other the meanings of words. Don't give any more help than this: sooner or later someone will see what has gone wrong.
	2 Ask the students, working individually or in pairs, to put the text right.
	3 Get them, in groups of 8–12, to compare and discuss their versions of the text.
	4 Give out the unscrambled texts.
NOTE	If you have access to a computer and printer, then not only can you get the computer to scramble the text for you, but you could produce differently scrambled versions for each student or group. The following short Basic program for BBC micro + Epson FX-80 can be easily adapted to most computer–printer combinations.

```
 10 lines=14: DIM text$(lines): INPUT"number of copies: "copies
 20 FOR N=1 TO lines: READ text$(N): NEXT N
 30 :
 40 FOR M=1 TO copies
 50   FOR N=1 TO lines: swap=RND(lines)
 60     T$=text$(N): text$(N)=text$(swap): text$(swap)=T$
 70       NEXT N
 80   VDU2: REM Turn printer on
 90   FOR N=1 TO lines: PRINT text$ (N): NEXT N
 100   VDU1,12,3 : REM eject page: turn printer off
 110   NEXT M
 120 END
 130 :
 140 DATA A railway worker at a
 150 DATA Midlands station was being
 160 ... etc
```

To use text prepared on a word-processor, write it as an ASCII file (without any special control characters), put the number of lines at the head of the file on a separate line, and rewrite program lines 10–30 thus:

```
 5 INPUT "number of copies: "copies
10 *EXEC < text file name >
20 INPUT""lines: DIM text$(lines)
30 FOR N=1 TO lines: INPUTLINE""text$(N): NEXT N
```

SAMPLE TEXTS

Scrambled text

A railway worker at a
secret Army document that
believed to have been found
fell into the hands of the
Provisional IRA.
The intelligence report on
night about the theft of a
Midlands station was being
disappeared after being posted
by thieves who rifled 14 mail-
to an Army officer. It was
the strength of the terrorists
questioned by detectives last
bags destined for London.

Original text

A railway worker at a
Midlands station was being
questioned by detectives last
night about the theft of a
secret Army document that
disappeared after being posted
to an Army officer. It was
believed to have been found
by thieves who rifled 14 mail-
bags destined for London.
The intelligence report on
the strength of the terrorists
fell into the hands of the
Provisional IRA.

[*The Daily Mail*]

Scrambled text

killed by the Torrey Canyon
8,000 by the Torrey Canyon.
25,000.
4,500 birds were killed by the
accident may be as many as
cil says that the numbers
It is estimated that at least
Amoco Cadiz incident, and
The Nature Conservancy Coun-

Original text

It is estimated that at least
4,500 birds were killed by the
Amoco Cadiz incident, and
8,000 by the Torrey Canyon.
The Nature Conservancy Council says that the numbers
killed by the Torrey Canyon
accident may be as many as
25,000.

[*The Guardian*]

Scrambled text

Two of them, including the dead
when a social worker called five
until their secret was revealed two
80-year-old widow were gaoled at
Oscar-winning performance' by pos-
lecting her pension after her death
months after Mrs Lily Townsend's
Birmingham Crown Court yesterday.
death one of the women put on 'an
years later. The jury heard that
Three women who secretly buried an
woman's daughter, carried on col-
ing as the old woman asleep in bed.

Original text

Three women who secretly buried an
80-year-old widow were gaoled at
Birmingham Crown Court yesterday.
Two of them, including the dead
woman's daughter, carried on col-
lecting her pension after her death
until their secret was revealed two
years later. The jury heard that
when a social worker called five
months after Mrs Lily Townsend's
death one of the women put on 'an
Oscar-winning performance' by pos-
ing as the old woman asleep in bed.

[*The Guardian*, 21 June 1983]

B/12 Find the swapped words

This exercise doesn't suit all students. It seems to appeal to people
with puzzle-loving minds who enjoy an intellectual challenge. I
strongly dislike it myself, but make a point of trying to use it and other
activities of the same sort with groups I reckon will enjoy it. One of the
most natural and wrong-headed things in teaching is the way teachers
tend to choose activities *they* happen to like, regardless of student taste.
Why should the sieve of my likes and dislikes be the sole determinant
of what gets to my students?—*M.R.*

LEVEL   **Intermediate to Advanced**

TIME   **45–60 minutes**

PREPARATION   Choose two short passages with related themes and styles. Take out
6–12 words you want students to focus on from one passage and
replace them by words from the other, and vice versa. In class you will

need copies of the distorted passages and the originals. (Examples can be found below.)

IN CLASS

1 Give out one distorted text to one half of the class and the other to the rest. Ask the students to read through their texts individually, and to make what sense of them they can.

2 Then ask the class to form pairs: in each pair the students should have different passages. Tell them how the texts have been distorted, and invite them to sort out the muddle.

3 Give out the undistorted original texts.

SAMPLE TEXTS

A (distorted text)

Language manufacture and language distribution are fields of activity which are engaging a great and growing amount of human description and energy. Thousands upon thousands of people make a living by teaching languages, and millions of others generate scores of man-hours each, trying to learn. Every year large numbers of books and articles appear dealing with language instruction in all its goods. Some publishers derive a considerable part of their income from the sale of language failure, and other firms specialize in making success aids. Language instruction occupies a fair proportion of broadcasting terms in many countries, and development companies are beginning to catch up. There is every reason to think that all these people will go on increasing in volume and intensity for a long time to come.

B (distorted text)

The object of any industry is the teaching and learning of material aspects. We do not speak of the 'religion industry' or the 'philosophy industry'. The 'knowledge industry' was an apt attention of the educational and scientific establishment as viewed by most activities in the 1960s. It was the means by which a country might spend the manufacture and distribution of material goods. It would stand or fall in time of its success or failure in turning out those who could help in the formation of 'knowledge workers' in research and television.

A (original text)

Language teaching and language learning are fields of activity which are engaging a great and growing amount of human attention and energy. Thousands upon thousands of people make a living by teaching languages, and millions of others spend scores of man-hours each, trying to learn. Every year large numbers of books and articles appear dealing with language instruction in all its aspects. Some publishers derive a considerable part of their income from the sale of language courses, and other firms specialize in making teaching aids. Language instruction occupies a fair proportion of broadcasting time in many countries, and television companies are beginning to catch up. There is every reason to think that all these activities will go on increasing in volume and intensity for a long time to come.

(Paul Christopherson, *Second Language Learning*, Penguin 1973)

B (original text)

The object of any industry is the manufacture and distribution of material goods. We do not speak of the 'religion industry' or the 'philosophy industry'. The 'knowledge industry' was an apt description of the educational and scientific establishment as viewed by most people in the 1960s. It was the means by which a country might generate the manufacture and distribution of material goods. It would stand or fall in terms of its success or failure in turning out those who could help in the formation of 'knowledge workers' in research and development.

(R. M. Hutchins, *The Learning Society*, Pall Mall Press 1968)

B/13 Who said what?

LEVEL

Intermediate to Advanced

TIME

15–30 minutes, or as homework

PREPARATION

1 Choose two short texts giving markedly different views on the same subject. Select 5–8 phrases or sentences from each, and recombine them in one composite text, using linking phrases where necessary. Underline the sections of original text.

2 Make copies of all three texts for each member of the class. (See the example texts below.)

IN CLASS

1 Give out a copy of the composite text to each student.

2 Tell the class how the text was created, and ask them to decide which of the underlined phrases or sentences are from original text **A**, and which from text **B**.

3 Give out copies of the original texts.

4 Ask them to make a short statement of each writer's point of view.

SAMPLE TEXTS

Original texts

A A state that tries to do for people what they should do for themselves is an evil state. It is both foolish and wicked to take money away from hard-working, thrifty citizens and give it to those who are idle and incompetent. If our society is ever to improve, then people must learn to be responsible: when times are good, they should save their money for when times are bad.

B In any society, however advanced, there are always people who are too weak, or too sick, or simply too unlucky to be able to take care of themselves and their families. In ancient times, such people were allowed to suffer and even to die. Let's hope that in these more enlightened days the state, that is to say society as a whole, will continue to look after its weaker members.

Composite text

[A state that tries], [in these enlightened days], [to do for people what they should do for themselves], [is an evil state]. [It is both foolish and wicked] [to take money away from hard-working, thrifty citizens] [and give it to those] [who are too weak, or too sick, or simply too unlucky] [to be able to take care of themselves and their families]. [If our society is ever to improve], [then people must learn] [to suffer and even to die]: [when times are good], [they should save their money for when times are bad].

B/14 Patchwork text

LEVEL | Elementary to Advanced

TIME | 20–40 minutes

IN CLASS | Ask the students, in groups of 2–4, to riffle through a poetry anthology and select lines at will. From these they should construct the opening paragraph of a novel.

EXAMPLES | *Yes, I remember Adlestrop—you would know him if you saw him for his eyes are sunken in. Just for a handful of silver he left us in the licorice fields at Pontefract, with a cargo of Tyne coal. Someone had blundered. I was weary and ill at ease. I thought, 'How paltry, how vulgar, what a mean act!' He returned before the dawn with his shirt and tunic torn, a sadder and wiser man. 'Is there anybody there?' he said. 'I am here at the gate alone.' But answer came there none.*

I shot the Albatross, and that has made all the difference. With silence and tears, we buried him darkly at dead of night. I swore—but was I sober when I swore?—he had softly and suddenly vanished away. I cried for madder music and for stronger wine, with beaded bubbles winking at the brim: 'My nerves are bad tonight. Yes, bad. Stay with me.' My father and my mother look'd at each other with a wild surmise; and gracious! how Lord Lundy cried.

(*The New Statesman*, 28 October 1983)

VARIATION | Instead of using an anthology, students can be invited to construct their texts from fragments of coursebooks, pattern sentences, etc. This is particularly suitable for elementary and intermediate students.

Acknowledgement
This was suggested by a competition in *The New Statesman*.

B/15 The words in your past

LEVEL

Elementary to Advanced

TIME

20–30 minutes

PREPARATION

Choose an emotionally charged text, like the one below. Only do this exercise in a group where there is plenty of mutual trust.

IN CLASS

1 Give out copies of the text, and ask the students to pick out six or seven words that they do not know, or give an instruction that focuses their attention on such words. In the text below, for example, ask them to look at all the words and phrases the writer uses to describe the way Prue treats her father: *exploit/victimize/take advantage of/play the little girl/see how far one can go/indulge*.

2 Ask them to think back to a period of their lives in which these words might fit, or for which they would be usefully descriptive.

3 Then ask the students to explain to one another, in pairs, how the words they have chosen fit or describe the period they have been thinking of.

VARIATION

Instead of asking the class simply to think back, ask them to draw a life line, and to label it first with dates and events, then with the words they have chosen from the passage.

SAMPLE TEXT

Daddy

Prue, putting the phone down, thought: I exploit him, I know I do. Or victimize him even. Now Mummy's different: hearing her voice just now there was no tug-of-war. Perhaps she prefers the boys, always did; or maybe she just accepts me as another grown-up woman. But Daddy I can take advantage of, even more than I used to. I simply can't avoid it: an irresistible impulse to play the little girl, to see how far I can go, to what length of self-indulgence he will allow me to sink. Gavin won't. Gavin won't put up with my nonsense. It simply doesn't appeal to him. He's tough.

It's extraordinary how quickly Daddy's forgiven me. Amazing, when I remember how angry he was. But he hasn't forgiven Gavin. Not at all. He can't even mention his name. I'm rather glad. That's wrong of me, I know. I should want them to like each other, but I don't, not if I'm really honest, and I always am, to myself. They both love me: that's enough. I don't really need them to love each other as well. And if they did, it might somehow diminish their love for me. I might not be quite such a special person for either of them if they drew together over me. They might see me too clearly. Or they might like each other too much, and where would I be then? Squeezed out by all those things men like to talk about, whatever they are, when they're alone. It's bad enough when Gavin's friends come round.

(Andrea Newman, *A Bouquet of Barbed Wire*, Triton Books 1969)

B/16 Cross-associations

LEVEL Elementary to Advanced

TIME 15–25 minutes

PREPARATION Choose and make copies of a short text. An example will be found below.

IN CLASS 1 Ask the students to read through the text and note down any words which they don't know, or which interest them. Ask them to find out the meanings, uses, etc. of the words.

2 Ask the group to build up a list of professions on the blackboard.

3 The students associate, in any way they wish, the words they have chosen with the professions.

4 Invite them in pairs to explain to each other their associations.

EXAMPLE The following list of professions was produced by one group:

electrician   joiner   accountant   bus-driver   baker
clergyman   foreman   butcher   teacher   apprentice
businessman   social worker   farmer   fisherman
politician

After reading the text below, the group formed the following associations:

beach, sand, sea	*teacher*	(because the beach is the best place for lessons)
paddock	*farmer* *butcher*	(connection with cattle)
squatting	*electrician* *joiner*	(from the position these people often have to work in)
horizon	*politician*	(because you can't see what is over the horizon, and you don't know the future you will get if a politician is elected)

VARIATIONS Other categories may be used to build the list of associations, e.g. furniture (chair, table, settee, wardrobe . . .), landscape features (hill, valley, wood, field, river . . .), famous people, people in the group itself.

SAMPLE TEXT **Goblins**

I never had clean beach sand to play on when I was a kid. In fact I never saw the sea before I was nine, so I used to build things out of mud. I can see myself now squatting in a corner of the big paddock, small and thin and brown in my patched khaki pants and shirt, lost in the creation of a remembered town. I always built in this same place, shaping walls of mud, doors and roofs of bark, and all around among untidy lumps of mud I made tower things from sticks above holes in the ground. In my mind's eye the houses were all painted dazzling white, and the big hotel on the corner was red brick with a cast iron balcony and corrugated iron roof. The other things were mines and slag heaps and pitheads, and stretching away from them I would see the spare desert scrub shimmering to a flat horizon and the whole land panting with heat under a bleached blue sky.

　　When the other kids found me they used to laugh and break up my mining town. Then I began building towns full of white goblins and I stamped them into the ground in a rage.

(Colin Johnson, *Wild Cat Falling*, Angus and Robertson 1965)

B/17 Keyword diagrams

LEVEL	**Elementary to Advanced**
TIME	**15–25 minutes**

PREPARATION　Select and present short poems. The examples below are:

a. (Intermediate): Roger McGough, *Penguin Modern Poets 10*, 1967
b. (Elementary): Tony, John, Malek, *Stepney Words I & II*, Centreprise Publications 1973
c. (Upper-Intermediate): Alan Bold, *In This Corner: Selected Poems, 1963–1983* (Macdonald 1983).

SAMPLE TEXTS

a.　There's something sad
　　about the glass
　　with lipstick on its mouth
　　that's pointed at and given back
　　to the waitress in disgust

　　Like the girl with the hair-lip
　　　　whom
　　　　　　no one
　　　　　　　wants
　　　　　　　　to
　　　　　　　　　kiss

b.　Alone he walks
　　He walks alone
　　He has no friends
　　And has no home
　　I noticed something from the back
　　He is alone because he's black

c. Cause and Effect

He thought before the war
Of conflicts, heroism, enemies
Who had to be crushed;
Causes that had to be fought for.

He had no time before the war
For bright skies, fields, the warm
Sun, his woman—only
Causes that had to be fought for.

I see him now after the war
In my lifetime. I notice his love
Of the sun, bright skies, fields, his woman:
Causes that have to be fought for.

IN CLASS

1 After the students have had a chance to read through the poem(s), invite them to express the meaning/structure/imagery in the form of keywords taken from the text and linked by some graphic device (e.g. arrows, or interlocking circles).

2 Ask the students, in groups of three, to explain to one another how and why they produced their diagrams.

EXAMPLES

In one group students produced these:

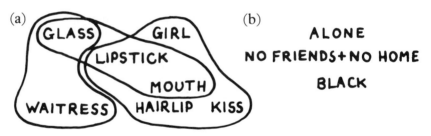

(a) GLASS GIRL LIPSTICK MOUTH WAITRESS HAIRLIP KISS

(b) ALONE NO FRIENDS+NO HOME BLACK

B/18 Be someone else

LEVEL

Intermediate to Advanced

TIME

30–40 minutes

PREPARATION

Choose a short text that is fairly rich in modern vocabulary and deals with a contemporary subject, as in the example.

IN CLASS

1 Ask the students to read through the text and note down words that they would consider particularly relevant to today's world.

2 The students should each select for themselves a historical role (e.g. an eighteenth-century peasant, an Egyptian Pharaoh, their own

grandmother/father), and spend a few minutes 'thinking themselves into' the role.

3 Ask the students to form pairs. One student should then read out his or her list of words one by one to the partner, who free-associates with the words *as if s/he were* the historical person chosen. After this the student then explains why these things came to mind.

4 The students then reverse roles and repeat the exercise.

EXAMPLE

From the text below, one student produced the list:

government	independence	concrete	black	beach
lunchtime	air-conditioned			

His partner, seeing herself as a villager in the 1850s in Japan, produced the following associations:

government	uncertainty, trouble
independence	not possible
concrete	don't understand
black	some foreigners are black
beach	we collect seashells for food
lunchtime	we eat to work
air-conditioned	don't understand

SAMPLE TEXT

The Prince Albert

Once the area around the main park had been residential and fashionable. But the people who had lived there had emigrated or had moved up to the hills; and the big private houses around the park had been turned into government offices or restaurants or business offices and later, with independence, into embassies and consulates. The Prince Albert was still, in spite of renovations and additions in concrete, and in spite of its internal iron pillars, like a grand old-fashioned estate house, an affair of timber and polished floors, with an open veranda-like lobby. Once it had been barred to black people and received tourists from the cruise ships coming down from the north, sightseers only in those days, before the beaches were discovered. Now it had an air of having been passed by; the tourists went to beach hotels; the Prince Albert had become local. The uniforms of doorman and waiters were not as crisp and starched as they would once have been; the building itself had begun to go in parts, with yielding floorboards in the lobby. At lunchtime the renovated air-conditioned bar was busy, with people who worked in the offices nearby; so that the atmosphere was casual, where once it had been exclusive. But to Jimmy the name, Prince Albert, still had a wonderful sound, still suggested privilege and splendour.

(V. S. Naipaul, *Guerrillas*, Andre Deutsch 1975)

Section C
Pictures and mime

C/1 Competitive dictation

LEVEL   **Beginner to Intermediate**

TIME   **15 minutes**

PREPARATION   Have ready, for your own use only, a list of the main parts of a car: bonnet, handbrake, headlight, steering wheel, roof-rack, windscreen wiper, etc.

IN CLASS   **1** Draw the minimal outline of a car on two large sheets of card. Stick these to the walls at either end of the room.

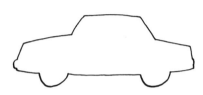

2 Divide the class into two groups, and ask each group to gather round one of the outline cars. Give each group a marker pen.

3 Shout out the first item on the list you have prepared. Each team has to write the word on the appropriate part of the car, and draw the item in if it is missing.

4 Ask the two teams to compare labelling, spelling, etc.

N.B. If you have a large class, you may want to have more than two teams working, each with its own outline.

VARIATION   Instead of drawing, the team can be asked to build the car with people. You shout out *wheels* and four people take up rounded crouching positions as wheels. You shout out *bumper* (or *fender* if you are teaching US English), and two people lie down in front of and behind the two sets of wheels, etc. Once the car has been built with people, you go up and ask the 'parts' to identify themselves: *What are you?—I'm the number-plate.*

Acknowledgement
We learnt this dictation technique in a seminar held at the University of Strasbourg.

C/2 Notion pictures

LEVEL   **Beginner to Middle-Intermediate**

TIME   **20–30 minutes**

PREPARATION   Choose a concept like *joining*, *water things*, or *protection*. Take a large dictionary with you to class, especially if English is not your mother tongue.

IN CLASS

1 Exemplify the chosen concept by drawing: for *joining* this might be, say, a hinge and a priest marrying two people.

2 Ask the students to draw as many things and people *that join* as they can. Let them work either on their own or in pairs.

3 Once the students have got a good number of drawings down on paper, and not before, ask them to label their drawings. They can make use of each other's knowledge, of dictionaries, and of you as an informant.

4 Ask the students to stand up and work in pairs, showing their drawings and teaching their words to other people. When they have finished with one partner, they should move on to another, rather than cluster in larger and larger groups. Stop the exercise when each person has worked with about five partners.

EXAMPLES

When we have done this exercise with *joining* as the concept word, students have produced drawings of the following:

crowd	*river*	*dividing line*
audience	*apex*	*swimming pool*
engagement ring	*bread and butter*	*electric plug*
cocktail	*border*	*handcuffs*
bridge	*comma*	*shelf*

With *water things* as the concept word, students have produced drawings of the following:

sprinkler	*spirit level*	*tap*
octopus	*starfish*	*well*
hosepipe	*whale*	*river*
estuary	*irrigation*	*spring*
gumboots	*umbrella*	*bath tub*
goggles	*water meter*	

C/3 Machines and scenes

The exercises outlined below may be used in any situation involving the drawing and labelling of pictures, diagrams, plans, maps, etc.

LEVEL

Elementary to Advanced

TIME

30–40 minutes

PREPARATION

Make sure before you start that you are fully conversant with the words that may be called for by the students, so that you may supply them if asked. Have a dictionary handy in class.

IN CLASS

1 Find someone in the group who likes drawing and ask him or her to draw a given scene/machine/situation/process on the blackboard. Tell the artist to use the whole of the board.

2 Once the drawing has begun to take shape, get someone in the group with clear handwriting to come out and start labelling what has been drawn. This should be done with the help of the group. As teacher, you should supply a word only when asked to: i.e. act as informant only.

3 Tell the students to copy the board drawing into their notebooks and to write the words on the drawings: this makes more sense than writing lists of words.

4 The words now need to be used in a context beyond the picture. Three ways of doing this are suggested in the detailed examples that follow.

EXAMPLES

Some word areas that lend themselves to this activity

A Tell the artist to draw a *bicycle*. Follow steps 1, 2, and 3 above in order to familiarize students with the necessary vocabulary. Then ask the students to look at the illustration below and to jot down all the differences they can see between the two bikes there. Ask the students to form pairs and compare the differences they have found—this will encourage oral production of the words being learnt.

Photocopiable © Oxford University Press

B Tell the artist to draw people working on a *building site*, with houses at different stages of completion. After doing steps 1, 2, and 3 above, ask the students a question such as 'Can the plasterer work on the house before the bricklayer?' Then tell them to organize themselves into a line across the classroom representing the time sequence in which building workers work on a house. Each student (or pair of students in a large class) is to assume the role of one type of worker. You should take no part in this organization, except to keep the speaking in English.

C Tell the artist to visualize the *dashboard and controls of a car*, as seen from the back seat, and to draw them. After the group has followed steps 1, 2, and 3 above, put two chairs out in front of them, side by side. Then invite one student to sit on one chair and play the part of a driving instructor, while you sit beside him or her and play the part of a slow pupil: show nervousness, and ask the instructor what each control is and what it is for. Then ask the whole class to act out the learner–instructor scene simultaneously in pairs.

As a follow-up activity, in a later class, ask the pairs to continue the scene into the first stages of a driving lesson: moving off and coming to a stop.

C/4 Build words into a picture

LEVEL **Beginner to Advanced**

TIME **15 minutes**

PREPARATION Choose twelve words from the next unit you are going to teach in the coursebook. They should be new words.

IN CLASS 1 Tell the group that they are going to draw a picture incorporating some of the new words from the next unit. The students should work independently of each other.

2 Tell them the first word, either explaining its meaning in English, paraphrasing it with a known word, miming it, or translating it. They make a drawing representing it. Give them the second word and explain/translate it. They continue the picture, incorporating the second word/idea. In this way they build each of the twelve words into one picture.

3 Say the words again slowly, and ask them to *write* each word over its representation.

4 Ask the students to compare their pictures.

C/5 Elephants

This exercise may at first sight seem strange. So it should, as it uses the principle of 'making strange' what is familiar. Having to place the words from your list on the elephant forces you to look at them from a new angle. It makes them strange. The exercise provides an excellent opportunity for peer-teaching, both of subject-matter and of lexis.

LEVEL **Elementary to Advanced**

TIME **40–50 minutes**

IN CLASS 1 Ask each student to write down a list of 8 to 12 words that are central to his or her profession, or to a hobby or interest.

2 Ask the students to draw a picture of an animal, machine, etc. All the students should draw the same subject: choose something which is clear, easy to draw, and which has recognizably distinct parts (e.g. elephant, cat, bicycle).

3 Ask each student to label the picture with the terms on the list: where to put the words on the picture is up to the student.

4 Form the students into small groups. They should in turn give short speeches on their chosen subjects, using their labelled picture as a visual aid.

EXAMPLE   One student who worked in photolithographic printing produced this elephant:

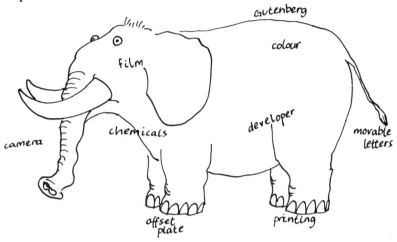

C/6 Coins speak

The spatial attributes of even abstract words can be powerful for many people. After an introductory session, the following exercise can be repeated many times during a course with whatever vocabulary happens to be under consideration.

LEVEL   **Elementary to Advanced**

TIME   **15–25 minutes**

PREPARATION   1 Assemble a collection of identical small objects, such as counters, coins, buttons: you will need around ten per student. You will also need one sheet of white paper for each pair of students.

2 Prepare an introductory list of words with a strong spatial or hierarchical sense for the students to practise on, e.g.

> *airport   beach   village   field   forest   school   garage*
> or *class   crowd   regiment   queue   party   club   junta*

3 Prepare a list or lists of words you would like the students to work on: these should be words of a strong emotional or controversial content, e.g.

> *guilt   independence   innocence   revenge   contradiction*
> *ingratitude   age   stability   sadness   hostility   death*

IN CLASS   1 Ask the students to form groups of 3–4.

2 Give them your list of spatial/hierarchical words. They should check their comprehension of all the words by using dictionaries, or asking you or each other.

3 Give each group a pile of 15–25 counters or coins, and a sheet of plain white paper to arrange them on.

4 Ask one student in each group to select a word from the list and then, without saying which word s/he has chosen, to represent the word by means of an arrangement of counters or coins on the paper.

5 When the first student has done this, the others in the group should try to guess which word was selected.

6 After each member of the group has selected and represented one word from the introductory list, introduce the second set of emotional words and ask them to continue working on them. Stop the exercise after two or three more rounds.

EXAMPLES

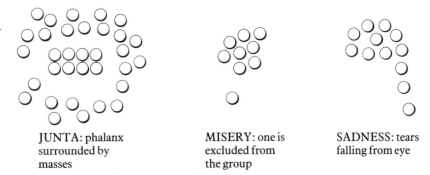

JUNTA: phalanx
surrounded by
masses

MISERY: one is
excluded from
the group

SADNESS: tears
falling from eye

VARIATIONS

1 After the introductory stage, ask the students to write their own lists of words that are important or exciting or disturbing for them, and to work in pairs on these.

2 The exercise can equally well be used as a pre-reading exercise. It then has the double value of exploring vocabulary from the text, and getting the readers to think through their own ideas and prejudices before reading. In the following text, the italicized words would be given to the class before they were encountered in the text:

While preparing for his weekly radio broadcast, Mr Reagan performed a routine test to check microphones for voice level. It came as a surprise when the President was heard to *intone*: 'My fellow Americans, I am pleased to tell you that I have signed *legislation* to *outlaw* Russia for ever. We begin *bombing* in five minutes.'

A Democratic Party spokesman commented: 'It is incredible that the President would joke about *war* with the Soviet Union. The comment reflects the *insensitivity* consistently shown by the man charged with leading the *free* world in the search for peace.'

C/7 Fishy adjectives

LEVEL   Intermediate to Advanced

TIME   30–40 minutes

IN CLASS Ask the students to follow the instructions of whichever worksheet you give them:

Worksheet 1

reflective   selective   deluded   paranoid   ostracized
redundant   self-centred   experienced   hostile   creative
diffident   easily influenced   out-of-place   gullible
marginal   anti-social   different   troubled   ill-at-ease
discriminating   out of her/his depth   victimized   edgy
deviant   condescending   intolerant   sent to Coventry
unemployed   questioning   confused   ill   in a dilemma
delinquent   responsive   proud   irresponsible   disruptive
divided   subversive   too big for his/her boots

1 If you were one of the fish in the shoal, which one would you be? Put a tick by it.

2 What three things might you say to the rest of the fish in the shoal about the fish in the bottom left-hand corner? Write your answers:

_____

_____

_____

3 Pick 10–15 adjectives and phrases from the list above, or from your head, to describe the fish that is out of the shoal. Look up any words from the list you don't know, or ask your neighbour.

4 Work in pairs with several different people in the group to find how and why they chose their adjectives.

5 Talk to your partner about anyone you know who is like the fish in the bottom left-hand corner, and about how that person shows it.

Worksheet 2

1 Give all these fish nicknames and write them down.

2 Which fish would you most like to be?

3 Which fish would you most hate to be?

4 Jot down ten adjectives to describe the fish you like most, and ten to describe the one you like least.

5 Compare your answers with your neighbours'.

Photocopiable © Oxford University Press

Acknowledgement
We learnt this exercise from Lou Spaventa.

C/8 Picture gallery

LEVEL

Elementary to Advanced

TIME

35–50 minutes

PREPARATION

Collect magazine pictures with a strong direct impact, visually uncluttered—portions are often more useful than whole pictures. Select enough pictures for each member of the class to have two. Make a varied selection. Take Blu-Tack to class.

IN CLASS

1 Split the class into two equal groups, one at each end of the room. Spread out half the pictures for one group and half for the other group.

2 Ask each student to choose a picture. They must not show the pictures to anyone in the other group. Remove any unchosen pictures.

3 Ask the students to write clearly on a piece of paper twelve words suggested by the picture they have chosen. BAN ADJECTIVES.

4 When everyone has finished, take away each student's picture and ask everyone to lay out their sheets of words at their end of the room.

5 Ask the students to change ends. Each should choose one list from those written by the other group.

6 Ask them to read their word lists and then to write a short paragraph describing the picture they imagine behind the words.

7 When they have done this, put up the pictures around the walls, and ask the students to look round for the picture that best corresponds to the list they have worked from, and to put up their paragraph and the word list next to it.

8 Invite the students to go round and look at the pictures and read the compositions.

EXAMPLE

A student in one group chose this picture, a detail cut from a magazine advertisement: the skin on a woman's stomach glistening with beads of moisture; her well-manicured hand is on her stomach, above the navel; a fine gold chain encircles her stomach. The student wrote this list of words suggested by the picture:

> finger   smooth skin   bath   red nails   woman   chain
> stomach   water   play   hair   navel

A student from the other group wrote this paragraph, suggested by the word list:

> A woman was lying in the bath. She has smooth skin. You can see her stomach and she was playing with a chain and you can also see her nails which reflect your eyes.

C/9 The picture behind the story

LEVEL

Elementary to Advanced

TIME

20–30 minutes

PREPARATION

Choose a painting or a strong photograph that makes you think of a story. Work the story out in your head and prepare to tell it in English. Don't write notes. The story should be derived from the picture but should *not* describe it.

IN CLASS

1 Tell your students you were looking at a painting/photo when a story came into your head. Tell the story.

2 Now ask the students to imagine the picture that inspired the story, and draw it.

3 Let them compare pictures and explain how they relate to the story.

4 Show the original picture.

Acknowledgement
We learnt this idea from Andrew Wright.

C/12 Better geography

EL

Beginner to Intermediate

E

20 minutes

CLASS

1 Ask the students to draw a map of their own country.

2 Students work in pairs to improve the geography of their country. This may mean changing its shape, taking features away, adding others. It might mean moving it to somewhere else in the world.

3 Ask the pairs to label features added or taken away, e.g. *volcano, large city, inland sea, peninsula*.

4 The pairs get together in sixes and compare the changes they have decided on.

The exercise is excellent for teaching terms in physical geography via creative thought: it capitalizes on the regressive, fantasy desire in us for a god-like power over the physical world.

C/13 Silent teaching from pictures

EVEL

Beginner

IME

20–30 minutes

REPARATION

Find a poster of a setting (room, station, etc.), or of a person, or of a scene: choose a simple, uncluttered picture large enough for details to be clearly visible from the back of your classroom. Decide which words you are going to teach from the poster, and print them in large letters on slips of paper. Provide yourself with Blu-Tack and a pointer, and a number of blank slips.

N CLASS

1 Put the poster up on the wall. Take the pointer and silently outline the first object you wish the students to name. Do the outlining very deliberately: this ensures that everybody is focusing and thinking.

2 Using eye contact and gesture, invite the students to name the object outlined. Do not speak.

3 If the correct word is given by the student, stick up the corresponding label on the picture.

If no one offers the right word, stick up a blank slip of paper on the picture and pass on to the next object to be named.

If students offer words in other languages that have no similarity to the English word, make clear, negative, but sympathetic gestures.

If a student offers a word that is partly right in form or pronunciation,

C/10 Listening in colour

LEVEL Elementary to Advanced

TIME 15 minutes

PREPARATION Choose a brightly coloured painting or poster in which the
of action. It should not be too complicated. Prepare to des
picture without mentioning any colour.

IN CLASS 1 Put the picture/poster up somewhere the group can't see
them that the picture is highly coloured, but that they will
imagine the colours for themselves. Then describe the pictu
spatial detail, but without mentioning any colour.

2 Ask people to tell the class which colours they saw in thei
They should be as specific as possible.

3 Show the group the picture: a general discussion may ens
which such points as these may come up:

– how the painter felt while painting it
– what kind of painter it might have been
– what kind of room it would suit
– would you like it in your house?

Acknowledgement
This idea appeared in an article by Malgorzata Szwaj in *Mode
Teacher* early in 1984. It belongs to a family of visual ideas pu
by Andrew Wright.

C/11 Filling a landscape

LEVEL Beginner to Advanced

TIME **3 minutes** in the first class, **10 minutes** in the second

PREPARATION Choose a picture with strong contrasts, such as a Breughel snow
that will photocopy clearly. Make a copy for each student.

IN CLASS Give out the copies. For homework, ask the students to write on
picture any words it suggests. These may be labellings of feature
are there, or they may be words suggested by the feel and mood o
picture. Encourage students to use dictionaries to find the words
want. Tell them they must be willing to teach any new words they
used.

IN THE SECOND CLASS Put the students in fours to compare the words they have found: a
of peer teaching will follow.

signal this and encourage him or her to hypothesize: the Silent Way finger-syllabification* method is well suited to this end.

4 When you have worked through all the words you wish to teach, focus attention on the blank slips of paper stuck on the picture. Ask the students to find out the words needed, using dictionaries. Then continue as in steps (2) and (3) above. As a last resort, name the object yourself.

5 Ask the students to re-draw the picture in their notebooks and to label the objects in it, writing the names on the objects.

IN A LATER CLASS

To revise the words, stick the poster up *back to front*, or put up an empty sheet of paper the same size, and invite a student to come out and stick the word labels on in the right places, with help from the rest of the class.

VARIATIONS

1 A group member comes to the board and draws a picture. The teacher then works on it in the Silent Way mode.

2 Students draw pictures for each other in pairs, labelling features in the pictures drawn by their partners, using a dictionary when necessary.

Acknowledgement

The above technique was devised by Caleb Gattegno (*Teaching Foreign Languages in Schools—The Silent Way*, Educational Solutions Inc. 1972).

Silent Way finger work: imagine I am trying to get you to produce the word for the numeral 4 in Modern Greek. I write 4 on the board and look at you silently and hopefully.

You:	*Four?*
I:	*(negative head shake)*
You:	*Quatro?*
I:	*(negative head shake)*
You:	*(. . . pause) . . . Tetra?*
I:	*(holding up and pointing to my thumb, eliciting the word again)*
You:	*Tetra?*
I:	*(doing a karate chop with my right hand) Syllables!*
You:	*Te-*
I:	*(looking happy, point to my thumb, eliciting the sound from you again)*
You:	*Te-*
I:	*(holding up left index finger, looking expectant, point to index finger)*
You:	*-tra*
I:	*(negative head shake, holding up index and middle fingers to show two more syllables are needed)*

The process goes on until you finally reach the target form TESSERA.

C/14 Mime your past

LEVEL

Elementary to Upper-Intermediate

TIME

10 minutes in the first class, **30–45 minutes** in the second

PREPARATION

Think of an incident from your past that you could briefly mime in class.

IN CLASS

Do the mime, then ask for a volunteer to prepare to do a mime based on some past experience. The mime should be ready for the next class.

IN THE NEXT CLASS

1 Invite the volunteer to do his or her mime in front of the group. Make sure everyone can see from where they are sitting.

2 The student does the mime again, stopping after each action. Ask the other students to say what s/he did. Here they may be trying to describe something that is clear to them, or they may be hypothesizing about what the student intended to convey.

Write the vocabulary generated by the mime randomly all over the board.

3 Pair the students and get **A** to tell the incident to **B**. Go round helping anyone who is stuck for words.

4 Now ask **B** to replay mentally the scene described by **A**, this time seeing it in colour, or focusing on the sounds of the action, or on the way in which things happened, and then to re-tell the story to **A** with these elements added. (See examples below.)

EXAMPLES

A: Here is an incident mimed by a Venezuelan student:
Manuel was drinking with a friend – he had to pick his drunken friend up off the floor – he put the man on his back – he carried him up the stairs to a bedroom – he put him to bed and pulled the covers over him – Manuel went to bed himself – he went to sleep – he woke up – he looked at his watch – he got up – he had a bad hangover – he also had a crick in his back that made him stoop forward – this condition lasted thirty days – then the pain changed and he went round bent to his left and with his head over to the left – all his friends called him 'five past six'.

B: Re-telling in colour: *Manuel, who was wearing a white suit and black hat, was drinking with his friend, a brown-skinned man with a red shirt . . .*

C: Re-telling with sounds: *Manuel was talking to his friend in a bar that was very quiet except for the sound of their voices. The friend got very drunk and fell to the floor with a thud . . .*

D: Re-telling with 'how' words: *Manuel was with a friend who drank heavily. At first they talked animatedly, but as they drank more, the friend spoke more and more indistinctly . . .*

C/15 Mime the words

LEVEL

TIME

PREPARATION

Beginner to Elementary

40–50 minutes in the first class and **40–50 minutes** in the second

Choose a simple story that some students may already know the gist of, such as a well-known fairy tale. For the sake of simplicity write out a version of the story in which most of the action and feelings are expressed from the protagonist's point of view, as in this example:

> *The little girl put on her coat*
> *she picked up her heavy basket*
> *she went out of the cottage*
> *and walked along the path*
> *she looked up at the green trees*
> *she listened to the birds singing*
> *she whistled happily*
>
> *Suddenly she saw a beautiful flower*
> *she smiled and knelt down*
> *then she picked up the flower*
> *she looked up*
> *and saw a big bad wolf with long ears and long teeth*
> *she screamed and ran away*
>
> *She walked and walked and walked*
> *she walked and walked and walked*
> *she got very tired and very hungry*
> *then she saw her grandmother's cottage*
> *she knocked three times on the door*
> *a deep voice said 'Come in, my dear!'*
> *she opened the door and went in*
>
> *The little girl saw an old lady in bed*
> *the old lady had a bonnet on her head*
> *but she had long ears and long teeth . . .*

IN CLASS

1 Get the students sitting comfortably: they should be relaxed and free of bags and writing materials. You also should be seated.

2 Read the story through twice at slow story-telling pace. Offer no explanations.

3 Get the students to stand up. If possible, clear away the furniture. Then ask the students to form up one behind the other in a large circle round the room. Tell them you are going to read the story again, this time sentence by sentence, and ask them to mime what they understand has happened. They should stay in the circle and walk or run behind the person in front when the story requires it.

4 Read the first sentence of the story. In the example given above, one or two students are likely to start miming putting on a coat.

5 Read the same sentence again, so that other students can imitate the mime. This will plant the idea that when they do not know words or

phrases in the story they can arrive at them by watching the mime of others. (If no one understands the sentence you have read, then mime it yourself slowly. If the students have had only 30–50 hours of English, there will be a number of sentences and words they will not understand: in each case, mime the actions yourself. Do not wander off into explanation or paraphrase.)

6 Go through the whole story like this, sentence by sentence, without hurrying the pace. Then repeat the process, the students miming on each occasion.

7 Ask the students to sit down where they can see the blackboard. Invite one student to come out and write up the main content words in the first part of the story as you dictate them: while the 'secretary' writes on the blackboard, the others should advise on spelling. Such a dictation, in the example story given, might run:

put on	*coat*	*picked up*	*basket*	*went out*	*cottage*
walked	*path*	*looked up*	*trees*	*listened to*	*birds*

IN THE NEXT CLASS

1 Revise the story by reading it again sentence by sentence and having the students mime it, as in the first class.

2 Ask the students to get into pairs.

3 Ask one member of each pair to tell the story to the other as best s/he can, right through to the end. (Some will make heavy weather of this, but at this level of language learning, that's quite all right.)

4 Now ask the second member of each pair to re-tell the story, seeing it in colour and adding colour words as s/he goes along, e.g. 'The little black girl put on her blue coat.' (See C/10.)

Acknowledgement
We learnt the idea of listening comprehension leading to mime from Sue Jennings, *Remedial Drama*, Pitman 1973. The 'seeing in colour' exercise is suggested by Viola Spolin in *Improvisation for the Theatre*, Pitman 1973.

Section D
Word Sets

D/1 Word profiles

LEVEL   **Intermediate to Advanced**

TIME   **10–15 minutes** in any one session

IN CLASS   1 Write up on the blackboard, as an example, three adjectives, e.g.

    old   grey   expensive

Then suggest a few things which are all these, such as a Rolls Royce, a castle, the Prime Minister, and invite the class to suggest more.

2 Invite a student to offer three more adjectives and ask the group to find 4–6 things that could be described by them.

3 Ask each student to write three adjectives on a slip of paper and to fold the paper. Collect up the slips and mix them in a hat or box. Then get one student to pick out a slip at random, open it, and write the adjectives up on the board.

4 Ask the students, working individually, to produce a list of things described by the new set of adjectives.

5 Get the students into groups of 4–7 to compare and explain their lists.

IN LATER CLASSES   This exercise can be repeated throughout a course, provided that it is not overdone in any one session. Instead of adjectives, they may try verbs or adverbs:

    (things which) bend   creak   rot
    (people who move) slowly   jerkily   quietly

D/2 Intelligence test

LEVEL   **Beginner to Intermediate**

TIME   **10 minutes**

IN CLASS   1 Put up the following words on the blackboard:

    pliers   hammer   nail   saw

2 Ask the students to write down the odd one out and give their reason(s). When they have done this, ask for their suggestions. Then tell them that the 'right' answer is *pliers*, because it is the only one with two legs. If there are many 'incorrect' answers, a discussion on the validity of such tests might well ensue.

3 Now ask the group to make as many sets as possible, using two or more of the items in the list.

EXAMPLES

all metal: nail   hammer   pliers
aggressive/active: pliers   saw   hammer
nail set: nail   hammer   pliers
could be verbs/are grammatically singular: hammer   nail   saw
tools: hammer   pliers   saw
one syllable: nail   saw
-er ending (agent form): hammer   pliers
Germanic origin: hammer   saw   nail

Acknowledgement
This type of exercise has previously been used in *Mazes*, by M. Berer and M. Rinvolucri, Heinemann 1981/Hueber 1985.

D/3 Differences

LEVEL

Intermediate to Advanced

TIME

15–25 minutes

PREPARATION

Prepare a list of 10–12 words which refer to very similar, but nevertheless distinct, objects. Here is an example of such a set:

pen   telescope   bullet   scroll   cigarette   telegraph pole
bicycle pump   log   car aerial   pencil   rolling pin   lipstick

Put each word on a separate card. With a large class you may need two or three identical sets, as each student will need to have a card. Take Blu-Tack to class.

IN CLASS

1 Give each student a word card. Working individually, each student now writes on a separate sheet of paper two or three sentences describing the object on the card, but *not its use*. Ask the students not to look at each other's cards.

2 As they are writing, take their cards and stick up the complete set(s) round the walls.

3 Take in the students' sheets and shuffle them. Give them out to the students, making sure that no one receives his or her own sheet. Ask them to match the descriptions they now have with the words round the walls, and put the descriptions up next to the words.

4 The students circulate and read the matched words and their descriptions.

5 Group the students in threes and ask them to choose 3–4 items from the word set, and then to discuss the differences between these words.

VARIATION

Here is a set of 'concept words' you could work with in the same way:

trust   non-aggression   friendship   co-operation
federation   partnership   alliance   companionship
collaboration   love   sympathy   harmony

D/4 Unusual word families

We are all familiar with lists of words that teachers think ought to go together. All the words round the dining table in Spanish, for example: *cuchillo, mesa, tenedor, vaso, cucharra. . .* Precisely because such lists are so easy to achieve, they have very little mnemonic value. They are too yawningly obvious. Below we offer suggestions for more challenging ways of building up gripping word categories: gripping because it is the *student* who has built up the word family in each case.

LEVEL   **Elementary to Advanced**

TIME   **10 minutes** for most of the suggestions below

IN CLASS   Use only one of these student-directed suggestions in any given lesson:

A Work in pairs and list things found in an office but *not* in a home.

B Besides the sex differences, how can you tell your father and mother apart? List the most salient physical and emotional differences. Do the work alone, then explain your list to a partner you trust.

C Work with a partner. List the differences between your car/bicycle and hers/his.

D Here is a list of common verbs:

clean   listen   heat   taste   squeeze   push   tap   open

Work in pairs and think of three typical doers of each action and one atypical one: e.g.

> *Clean:* typical: laundryman/painter/dentist
> atypical: tramp

Compare your lists with those of other pairs.

E Work together in fours. One person should think of a place, building, or room, and tell the others three things that would be found there. The others should then try and guess the place. For example:

> Student A *(thinking of a library)*: shelf   sunblind   catalogue.
> Student B: A lawyer's office?
> Student C: A supermarket?
> Student A: Here's an extra word: *book* . . .

D/5 Three little words

LEVEL   **Elementary to Advanced**

TIME   **10–20 minutes**

PREPARATION   Select twenty words from the next unit in your coursebook. Half of them should already be known. Make four lists, each of five words, and make sufficient copies of each for one quarter of the class.

IN CLASS

1 Divide the class into groups of four. Give out the lists of words so that each person in a group receives a different list. Tell them not to show their lists to the other members of the group. Ask students to use dictionaries to look up words they do not know or are not sure of.

2 Ask each group to split into two pairs, and explain the rules of the game: in each pair, **A** will think of a word on his or her list and say another word that could be associated with it. **B** must try and guess what **A**'s word is. If **B** guesses wrongly, **A** gives another associated word. **B** is allowed up to three guesses. While **A** and **B** are playing, the other pair observes and, if necessary, adjudicates. Pairs should alternate in playing the game until all the words have been used.

EXAMPLES

association		guess	
A:	*beer*	**B:**	*glass*
A:	*wine*	**B:**	*bottle*
A:	Yes!		
C:	*pope*	**D:**	*priest*
C:	*rope*	**D:**	*soap*
C:	*want*	**D:**	*hope*
C:	Yes!		

Acknowledgement
We learnt this game from a Dutch-language TV programme in Belgium.

D/6 Chains

LEVEL

Elementary to Advanced

TIME

20 minutes

PREPARATION

Prepare a card for each student. On each card write the name of one man-made object (e.g. sweater, book, sewing-machine).

IN CLASS

1 Divide the class into small circles (4–5 members). Give each student a word card.

2 Ask the students to look at the word on their card and either write in front of the word the name of something that went into the making of the object, or, following the word, to write the name of something that the object might become. For example, if the word was *sweater*, one might write *sheep* before it or *paper* after it.

3 Each student should then pass the card to his or her left-hand neighbour, who should again write a word before or after the two words now on the card, e.g. *grass sheep sweater*.

VARIATION   Instead of arranging the chain in a linear fashion, a tree could be built, e.g.:

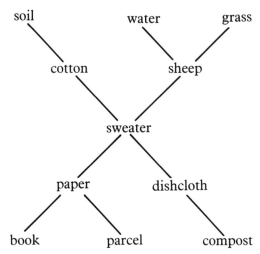

D/7 Collecting collocations

LEVEL   **Intermediate to Advanced**

TIME   **5 minutes** in the first class, **30–40 minutes** in the second

PREPARATION   Collect enough newspapers and magazines to be able to give at least half of one to each student. A page or two is not enough for this exercise.

IN CLASS   Give each student a newspaper or half a newspaper. Ask them for homework to pick out adjective–noun combinations where at least one item is new to them, or else their juxtaposition is. Ask them to find six such combinations each and to prepare to teach their meanings to the rest of the class. This may well mean bringing in the context in which they found them. Stress that they must be able to teach their collocations clearly and briefly.

IN THE NEXT CLASS   1 Divide the board into eight columns and invite a student to put one of his or her combinations in the first two columns and to teach it to the class. Then ask the group to produce other nouns that combine well with that adjective. Suppose a student volunteers a combination such as *forthcoming event*. The columns might well look like this:

adjective	noun	noun	noun	noun	noun	noun	noun
forthcoming	*event*	*sale*	*marriage*	*issue*	*publication*	*strike?*	*debut*

If a person in the group comes up with a dubious combinational companion for *forthcoming* like *strike*, let the students thrash it out as far as possible among themselves—do not make a ruling for them, *ex cathedra*.

2 Invite different students to volunteer to teach one of their six combinations, until the board is full.

VARIATION 1

Many other combinations can be worked on, using the same method. Here are some of them:

noun – noun:	*tax burden*
	dancing master
adverb – adjective:	*unfortunately misleading*
	vastly complicated
adverb – verb:	*greatly to be regretted*
	inevitably flowed from
verb – adverb:	*vary greatly*
	replied huffily

VARIATION 2

Put a list of twenty nouns and ten verbs on the board. The students copy down the lists and supply each noun with a typical adjective and each verb with a typical adverb, e.g.

an eccentric *millionaire*

to kiss lovingly

Acknowledgement
We learned this technique from Mike Lavery, author of 'Lead-ins and Fadeouts' (unpublished manuscript), and wish to thank him for allowing it to appear in this book.

D/8 Adverb brainstorm

LEVEL

Elementary to Advanced

TIME

20–30 minutes

IN CLASS

1 Ask the students in groups of three to write down all the ways they can think of that people talk, e.g. *grumpily/softly/cheekily*. Tell them they have three minutes.

2 Have three groups of three come together and enrich each other's lists.

3 Say *Hello!* as flatly as you can. Ask the students how many different ways it could be said.

4 Ask a student to choose a particular way of saying *Hello!* and to say it that way to the rest of the group, who should then guess the appropriate adverb.

You can do this exercise with many different verbs, e.g. *walk/listen/ bake/sit/eye*.

Acknowledgement
We learnt this technique from Helen Green and Sally Dalzell of the Marble Arch Cooperative School, London.

D/9 Jumping round the circle

In one sense this is a vulgar, Skinnerian drill, but the movement and laughter redeem it.

LEVEL

Beginner to Intermediate

TIME

10 minutes

PREPARATION

Choose any set of nouns you want the students to work on, e.g
food: *cheese*   *salad*   *chicken*
sleep: *pillow*   *bed*   *yawn*
Put each word from the chosen set on a separate card. Each student will need a card, so you may have to make several sets.

IN CLASS

1 Give each student a word card.

2 Split your class into groups of 10–14 and ask them to check in the group that they understand the words they have been given.

3 Make an open space in the room so that each group can stand in an inward-facing circle. Ask each student to draw a circle round where s/he is standing in chalk, except for one person who goes and stands in the centre of the circle.

4 Ask each student to call out the word on his or her card, preceded by an adjective of his or her choice—so **A**, holding the word *salad*, might call out *green salad*. Ask them to call out their adjective–noun combinations in turn several times.

5 The person in the centre of the circle now calls out three or four of the adjective–noun combinations, previously proposed by the group members, as fast as s/he can. The people whose words are called out *must* change chalk circles and the person in the middle must also try to get into a chalk circle. This means that one person is always left without a circle: s/he now goes into the centre and calls out combinations.

Acknowledgement
Ken Sprague, the artist and psychodramatist, played this game with us as a warm-up to a socio-drama session.

D/10 Diagonal opposites

LEVEL Beginner to Intermediate

TIME 10 minutes

PREPARATION You will need a soft ball.

IN CLASS 1 Write up on the blackboard three or four words with clear opposites, e.g. *cold*, *sad*, *rise*. Ask the class to suggest opposites for them.

2 Add two or three words that do not have clear opposites, e.g. *ball*, *typewriter*, *Wednesday*. Suggest that by using the personal associations of words one can think of 'opposites' for these too—give an example (e.g. *ball—mouse* because both are cats' playthings—the one dead, the other alive).

3 Ask the class to form circles of 6–10 people. Give each group a ball. The first player takes the ball, shouts out a word, then throws the ball to another member of the circle. The second player shouts out an 'opposite', then a new word, and throws the ball to a third player. Let the game continue until twenty words have been dealt with.

Acknowledgement
We learnt this game from an internal publication brought out by Volkshochschule teachers of French in Lower Saxony, West Germany. Working on 'opposites' can also usefully be used for grammar practice: see *Grammar in Action* by C. Frank and M. Rinvolucri (Pergamon/ Hueber 1983).

D/11 Keywords

LEVEL Elementary to Advanced

TIME 30–45 minutes

PREPARATION Get copies of at least seven different books on a range of topics. If your class has 14 students, you will need two copies of each title; if 21, then three copies, etc.

IN CLASS 1 Ask the students to form groups of 5–7.

2 Give each group a pile of books. There should be one book for each student and each book should be different.

3 Each student takes one book and skims through it for one to two minutes, trying to work out its subject matter and flavour.

4 At the end of the time limit, ask the students to close the books and spend about two minutes writing down the subject matter and flavour in the form of keywords.

5 Ask the students to pass the books they have just skimmed to their neighbours, and to repeat steps (3) and (4) with the next books.

6 Continue the activity until each student in a group has skimmed and written keywords for each book.

7 Then ask the students, working together in their groups, to compare and discuss their lists of keywords.

NOTES

Although this activity is used here to focus on lexical items, it has a number of possible applications:

1 It can be used to simulate the processes that go on when one is choosing books in a library or bookshop.

2 It provides a useful introduction to skimming as a necessary reading skill.

3 It can give form to a situation where students are having to choose from among a number of books for closer study, as with project work, examination set books, etc.

D/12 An ill wind . . .

LEVEL

Intermediate to Advanced

TIME

20–30 minutes

IN CLASS

1 Ask the students to work in pairs. Their task is to decide which of these people would gain and which lose from a national rail strike. Who would both gain *and* lose?

miners	*rail union officials*	*the strikers*	*truck owners*
woodcutters	*the government*	*out-of-work truck drivers*	
black marketeers	*commuters*	*petrol station owners*	
free-lance mechanics	*rickshaw coolies*	*police*	*housewives*
street vendors	*airport baggage handlers*	*conscripts*	
rail blacklegs	*pensioners*	*commercial travellers*	*soldiers*

2 Ask the pairs to come together in groups of six and compare their lists.

VARIATION

You could ask your class to prepare such a list of possible gainers and losers for other kinds of crisis: *drought/bi-national war/earthquake/coup d'etat/general election/epidemic*.

You could then use their list with another, lower-level class. Most preparation done by teachers is a waste of time when it can be better and more profitably done by groups of students.

D/13 Classifying knowledge

LEVEL

Intermediate to Advanced

TIME

20–30 minutes

IN CLASS

1 Put the students in threes and ask them to rank the following types of skill/knowledge (a) for their usefulness in everyday life; (b) in terms of the value of qualifications that might be gained through acquiring such knowledge.

> *tooth care   soil chemistry   surgery   psychiatry   arithmetic*
> *micro-computing   knitting   geometry   plain cookery*
> *darning   league football   literary criticism   music*
> *nuclear physics   cordon bleu cookery   pop music*
> *servicing a motor car   ancient Greek   carpentry*
> *road safety   filling in tax forms*

2 Ask the threes to come together into nines and compare their rankings.

VARIATIONS

1 Ask the students to rank the following areas of knowledge according to their usefulness in helping someone to win a TV or radio general knowledge quiz:

> *medieval history   civil engineering   cookery   medicine*
> *criminology   car mechanics   literature   plumbing*
> *computer science   electronics   geography   modern history*
> *philately   cinema studies   science fiction   theology*
> *art history   physics   astronomy   mythology   musicology*
> *carpentry   astrology   sociology   political science*
> *biology   gardening   librarianship   communications science*
> *mathematics*

2 Which of the following professions would give the best background to such a quiz?

> *taxi-driver   nurse   bookseller   language teacher*
> *photographer   electrician   tax inspector   journalist*
> *film producer   stockbroker   accountant   coalminer*
> *insurance salesman   science teacher   veterinary surgeon*
> *novelist   farmer   footballer   boxer   systems analyst*
> *policeman   oilfield worker   meteorologist   bank manager*
> *dress designer   advertising executive   greengrocer*
> *pub landlord   foundry worker   optician*

Acknowledgement
Roger Gomm and Patrick McNeill (eds.), *Handbook for Sociology Teachers* (Heinemann 1982)

D/14 Category consequences

LEVEL   **Elementary to Advanced**

TIME   **20 minutes**

IN CLASS   1 Divide the class into groups of 4–8. Each group should sit in a circle.

2 In each group, each player should have a clean sheet of paper.

3 Each player writes across the top of the page a list of words (maximum 8) which for him or her form a category, and then passes it to the player on the left.

4 On receiving the list, the second player should write the name of the category s/he believes is exemplified, fold the paper so that the original list cannot be seen, and pass it to the next player.

5 The third player should then write a list of 5–8 words exemplifying the category named, fold the paper so that only the new list can be seen, and pass it to the next player, and so on, alternating lists and category names, until each player receives the paper s/he started with.

Acknowledgement
This game was thought up during a seminar at the British Council, Paris.

D/15 Charting words

LEVEL   **Elementary to Advanced**

TIME   **10–20 minutes**

PREPARATION   Compile a set of vocabulary with some unifying theme: for this activity you may well choose a set of words which you think the students will require for a discussion activity, or which you think may provoke a discussion.

IN CLASS   1 Put up the vocabulary in the form of a jumble or unordered list.

2 Allow the students to look at the words, think about them, and ask questions about meanings. Encourage the use of dictionaries.

3 When the students have had plenty of time to think about the words, ask them to organize the set into a net, tree, flow-chart, or similar diagram. Give minimal examples if absolutely necessary. This stage may be done by students working individually or in small groups: if the latter, insist on unanimity within each group.

4 Ask the students to display and explain their diagrams.

EXAMPLES   (a) (Intermediate students)   (b) (Intermediate group of three)

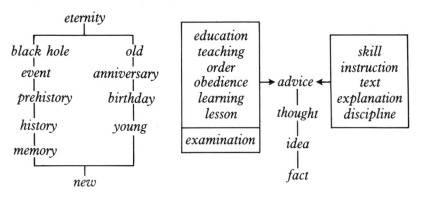

D/16 Role assignation

LEVEL   Elementary to Advanced

TIME   15–30 minutes

PREPARATION   Prepare a list of words that describe or denote people (e.g. professions, persons connected with health, education, money, etc., status terms, character terms) to give to the students on the blackboard or worksheets. Make sure that your list contains a mixture of familiar and unfamiliar terms. Thus, for an upper-intermediate class, you might use one of these lists:

(a) money people	(b) role verbs	(c) status terms★
banker	confront	boss
accountant	mediate	empress
moneylender	negotiate	leader
stockbroker	counsel	principal
bookmaker	warn	president
gambler	comfort	dictator
forger	lead	matron
cashier	guide	archbishop
tax inspector	advise	tycoon
economist	order	judge
financial journalist	manipulate	manager
wages clerk	deal	prime minister
speculator	interpret	mother superior
trader	communicate	chairman
investor	interview	headmistress

★These have been chosen from more or less the same status level: to mix levels would perhaps introduce an unwanted tension in the role-assignments.

IN CLASS

Ask the students, for homework, to work through the list with a dictionary or an informant.

IN THE NEXT CLASS

1 Divide the students into groups of 6 or 8. Write down and give to each group a set of words from the list: there should be as many words as there are people in the group.

2 Ask each student to write down the names of the other members of her/his own group (including her/himself), and to write against each name a word from the set which might fit them. E.g.

> Francine *confront*
> Norbert   *mediate*
> John *interview*
> Catherine *interpret*
> Mario *deal*

3 Ask the students in each group to pair off and tell each other how they have assigned the words within the group. They should then form new pairs until each student has spoken individually to each member of the group.

D/17 Specific purpose words

LEVEL

Elementary to Advanced

TIME

5 minutes in the first class, **30–40 minutes** in the second

IN CLASS

Tell the group that for homework you want them to get together a set of words for a particular area of English. The definition of the area is up to them. It could be the vocabulary needed for talking about a hobby or sport they have never practised in English, or for an area of their work. It could be words they would need to tell the story of a film to an English addressee or the words needed to describe a recipe. You could ask them to get together the vocabulary they would need to write a boring letter to an English-speaking pen-pal, or a different set for an exciting letter. The words might be those needed in a hypothetical situation, e.g.

– persuading English-speaking cannibals not to eat one
– advising a client on a new computer
– working as a doctor in an out-patients' clinic

Ask each student to come with 25 words at least and to be ready to explain the words.

<table>
<tr><td>IN THE SECOND CLASS</td><td>Ask the students to work in groups of four and teach each other the vocabulary sets they have compiled.</td></tr>
</table>

Acknowledgement

Virginia French Allen in *Techniques in Vocabulary Teaching* (OUP, New York 1983) writes of the teacher needing to decide the vocabulary areas the students work in. Her thoughts made us feel that maybe the student could do the deciding, the searching, and the teaching.

D/18 The egg exercise

<table>
<tr><td>LEVEL</td><td>Beginner to Advanced</td></tr>
<tr><td>TIME</td><td>20 minutes</td></tr>
<tr><td>IN CLASS</td><td>1 Ask the students, working on their own, to complete the following sentence stems in as many varied ways as they can: at least seven completions for each sentence.</td></tr>
</table>

An egg ....

Eggs ....

It's hard to .... *eggs* ....

2 Ask a student to come to the board and act as class secretary. The students shout out all the nouns and verbs they have used in their completions. Fill the board with the students' lexis.

3 In fours the students read out their sentences to each other.

Section E
Personal

E/1 An icebreaker

(For learning names at the beginning of a course)

LEVEL

Elementary to Advanced

TIME

10–15 minutes

PREPARATION

Decide on an area of vocabulary such as *containers, feelings, vehicles.*

IN CLASS

1 Get the students into groups of 10–15, if possible sitting in closed circles.

2 Invite student **A** to introduce him/herself by giving his or her true name and one item from the chosen area of vocabulary, e.g. with *containers*:

    A. *I'm Mario and I'm a flowerpot.*

Student **B** reports this and then continues in the same way:

    B. *He's Mario and he's a flowerpot; I'm Fukiko and I'm a milk-bottle.*

3 This goes on round the circle, with each student introducing all those who spoke before and then making a statement about him/herself.

Acknowledgement
We learnt this exercise type from Pfeiffer and Jones (eds): *Structured Experiences for Human Relations Training* (University Associates, La Jolla California 1978). The use of the exercise for grammar practice is outlined in C. Frank and M. Rinvolucri: *Grammar in Action* (Pergamon/Hueber 1983).

E/2 A job for a name

LEVEL

Elementary to Advanced

TIME

20–30 minutes

IN CLASS

1 Write up these English names on the board:

    George   Clint   Catherine   Sheila   Herbert   Alice
    Mary   William   Francis   Gertrude   Deborah

2 Pair the students and ask them which of these first names would be most appropriate for (a) a bank manager; (b) a pop star; (c) a trade union leader.

3 Put the pairs together in fours to exchange ideas.

VARIATIONS

1 Give out this list of jobs and ask the students to find first names in their mother tongue that fit the jobs:

publican   architect   printer   jockey   lawyer
rag-and-bone man   librarian   plumber   rat-catcher
shoe-shine boy   barber   undertaker   farmer   teacher
driving instructor   taxi-driver

2 Write up the names of the people in the group. Ask the students to decide on jobs for these names.

E/3 You give my talk

While speakers often impose subject matter on listeners, the listener seldom has the same privilege. Here the listener suggests the topic and guides its content by proposing a set of keywords.

LEVEL

Elementary to Advanced

TIME

5–10 minutes in the first class and **30–45 minutes** in the second

IN CLASS

1 Ask the students individually to list five topics they would like to hear a short talk on, and then in pairs to exchange lists.

2 Ask each student to choose and mark one item on her/his partner's list that s/he would be willing to talk on.

3 Students should give back the lists to their partners.

4 For homework, tell the students to prepare a vocabulary list for the topic their partners have elected to speak on.

IN THE NEXT CLASS

1 Ask the students to pair up as in the previous class and give their vocabulary lists to their partners.

2 Each student should now work individually on preparing a talk. It is not obligatory to use the words on the partner's list, but the list will provide some idea of the future listener's knowledge of and attitude towards the subject.

3 Ask one member of each pair to give his or her talk to the other.

4 Ask the listener in each pair to explain how s/he came to construct the vocabulary list, and what s/he would have said in giving the same talk.

5 Repeat the activity, with each listener now giving his or her talk.

E/4 Life keywords

LEVEL	**Elementary to Advanced**
TIME	**25–40 minutes**

IN CLASS

1 Ask the students what date it is today. Write it on the board. Ask them what the date was seven years ago. Put that on the board. Ask three or four people how old they were on that date, seven years ago.

2 Now ask the students to write down ten key emotional or idea words and phrases that sum up their lives *now* and a further ten to sum up their lives *then*.

3 Ask the students to pair off and explain the words and their significance to their partners. Have them change partners three or four times, not more, as this kind of talking is very tiring.

EXAMPLES

One person of 39 in this exercise came up with:

'Now' words	'Past' words
making new	*change*
letting free	*hitch-hiking*
conflict inside	*shadow theatre*
commitment	*commitment*
unease with work group	*Chile*
future	*break with mother*
retirement	
death	

Another of 18 had:

money	*marbles*
university	*friends*
family	*school*
friends	*music*
future	*father*
engagement	*mother*

E/5 Turn out your pockets

LEVEL	**Elementary to Upper-Intermediate**
TIME	**20–35 minutes** in the first class and **15–25 minutes** in the second

IN CLASS

1 Ask the students to list some or all of the objects in their handbags/wallets/pockets: ask the class to write their lists clearly.

2 When the lists are ready, ask the students to fold them and give them to you. Shuffle the lists and let each student pick one at random. No student should end up with his or her own list.

3 Ask the students to guess whose list they have and to tell the class why.

**IN THE NEXT
CLASS**

1 Ask each student to list the contents of the pockets or handbag of an imaginary person: they should list 10–12 objects.

2 Get them to exchange lists: each person then writes a thumb-nail sketch of the imaginary person whose list they have.

3 Ask them to stick the word lists and descriptions around the walls so that everyone can read them.

Acknowledgement
We learnt this exercise from Lou Spaventa. A similar one is found in G. Moskowitz: *Caring and Sharing in the Foreign Language Class* (Newbury House 1978).

E/6 Scars

LEVEL

Elementary to Upper-Intermediate

TIME

40–60 minutes

PREPARATION

Bring back to mind the story of a scar that you have or that a close relative of yours has.

IN CLASS

1 Tell the students your scar story. If it is about a scar of yours that is showable, let them see it.

2 Invite the group to think of how they got whatever scars they have. Give them a few minutes to bring their stories back to mind.

3 Ask a volunteer to tell his or her story. Help with words, and write any accident-related vocabulary up on the board, e.g. *wound, bandage, stretcher, stitches, operate*. Only write up words actually needed by the narrator.

4 Ask three or four more people to tell their scar stories to the whole class, and build up further vocabulary on the board.

5 If the class is a large one, now ask them to work in threes and continue telling scar stories, until everybody who wants to has told one.

6 Pair the students. Each student is silently to imagine a scar story for his or her partner. At this stage, remind them of the words on the board. Discourage them from writing.

7 Each student tells the partner the scar story about him or her.

VARIATIONS

There are many themes that can be used, though at different levels of intensity and involvement. If *scars* evoke short stories, for example, *hair* can produce autobiographical novels. (How was your hair when you were eight? Can you remember the first time you visited a hairdresser's? Have you ever dyed your hair? . . .)

Other themes for anecdotes that we have tried include *stairs*, *clothes*, and *houses*.

Acknowledgement
We learnt this exercise from Christine Frank.

E/7 Three of a kind

LEVEL	**Intermediate to Advanced**
TIME	**10–15 minutes**
IN CLASS	**1** Ask each student to write down the titles of three books that have affected them. Alternatively, they could choose three public figures, three towns, three languages, etc.
	2 Ask them to find and write down five adjectives to describe each.
	3 When they have done this, they should explain their choice of books and words to two partners.

E/8 Words my neighbour knows

LEVEL	**Intermediate to Advanced**
TIME	**20 minutes**
IN CLASS	**1** Divide the class into pairs.
	2 Ask each student to write a list of ten words which their partner

    a. should know
    b. should know but *doesn't*
    c. definitely *doesn't* know.

The partners must *not* communicate at this stage.

3 Then ask the pairs to check out the accuracy of the predictions.

Section F

Dictionary exercises and word games

F/1 The alphabet

LEVEL   Beginner to Intermediate

TIME   10–15 minutes

PERSONALITY TEST

For those familiar with the Roman alphabet, it is a rich source of association; for those who are still struggling with it, visual and auditory associations may be a powerful aid to learning. The following questions may be answered individually or in groups:

1 *b g h l k*: which are stronger?

2 *u* would be useful for bathing a baby. What could you use these letters for: *o e z t i*?

3 *w n h m v s*: which is the most comfortable?

4 Which of these would you most like as a picture in your living room: *j q r f*? Why?

5 *t* might be someone pointing into the distance. What do these remind you of: *d x y c o w*?

CALLIGRAPHY

1 Draw a cartoon portrait from each letter of the alphabet, e.g.

2 Choose eight letters of the alphabet and incorporate them in a scene.

LETTER SETS

Here are two ways of dividing the alphabet into sets. What criteria were used to make the categories? Can you think of any other ways?

1	a	b	f	i	o	q	r	(The names of the letters
	h	c	l	y		u		are pronounced similarly.)
	j	d	m			w		
	k	e	n					
		g	s					
		p	x					
		t	z					
		v						

2 AEFHIKLMNTVWXYZ   (The letters are made with straight lines only.)

BCDGJOPQRSU   (The letters include curved lines.)

SEQUENCES

1 Ask the students to stand up and arrange themselves in a line in alphabetical order. They can do this several times: by surnames, by first names, or by some other key, such as the names of their home towns.

2 Make sure each student has a dictionary. Put up at random 4–6 words on the blackboard. Ask the students to find the words in their dictionaries by turning as few pages as possible, and to write down a definition for each. (It may be useful to spend a little time beforehand on the use of the 'running heads' at the top of each page.)

3 Make packs of 20–30 word cards. You will need one pack for each group of 2–4 students. Ask the groups to sort the cards by first letter, then by second letter, etc. This can be made competitive by offering a prize for the first sorted pack.

F/2 Circle games

There is a host of word games that can be played in circles of 3–7 players. Here are some of them.

LEVEL

Beginner to Advanced

TIME

10–15 minutes

LETTER BY LETTER

Player **A** says a letter. Player **B** thinks of a word beginning with **A**'s letter and says its second letter. **C** thinks of a word beginning with the two letters already given and says its third letter, and so on round the circle. The person who, in saying a letter, completes a word, loses and must drop out (or lose a life). If a player, *on his/her turn*, thinks that the combination offered so far cannot lead to a word, s/he may challenge the previous player to say the word s/he is thinking of: if there is no such word, that player loses a life, otherwise the challenger is penalized. The game continues until only one player is left. For example:

A: *d*	**A:** *c*
B: *o* (→ *dog*)	**B:** *h* (→ *change*)
C: *l* (→*dole*)	**C:** *r* (→ *Christ*)
D: *l* (→ *dollar*)	**D:** *o* (→ *chromium*)
E: *That's a word!*	**E:** *That's not possible: what's your word?*
D loses a life.	**D:** *c-h-r-o-m-i-u-m*.
	E loses a life.

TAIL TO HEAD (1)

A thinks of a word and says it aloud. **B** has to say a word that begins with the last letter of **A**'s word, then **C** a word beginning with the last letter of **B**'s word, and so on round the circle until someone makes a mistake, or cannot find a word. (A time limit of, say, five seconds per player makes this more exciting.)

More difficult: **B** has to find a word beginning with the last two letters of **A**'s word, e.g.

> *table*   *LEmon*   *ONly*   *LYmph*   *PHarmacy* . . .

TAIL TO HEAD (2)

A thinks of a word and says it; **B** has to find a word beginning with the last *sound* of **A**'s word, e.g.

> *edge*   *join*   *noisy*   *evil*   *look*   *catch*   *cheese* . . .

THEME ALPHABETS

A chooses a category, states it, and names one member beginning with 'A', e.g. 'buildings: A is for Acropolis'. **B** must find a building beginning with 'B', e.g. 'B is for Bank', and so on round the circle. ('Hard' letters such as Q and X can be omitted if wished.)

LIPOGRAMS

A chooses a letter of the alphabet. S/he then gives a short sentence which must not contain that letter. The other player, in turn, must make similar 'lipograms'.

> **A:** *'S'. We're all in a circle.*
> **B:** *It may rain tomorrow.*
> **C:** *It's not raining now.*
> **D:** *Wrong! There's an 'S' in 'it's'.*

SETS

Find all the professions you can that start with S and end with R (*sailor, schoolteacher* . . .). Find all the verbs of sound containing the syllable *-ing* (*ring, sing, jingle* . . .).

TONIC SOLFA

Round the circle, each player must make a word containing one or more of the notes of the tonic solfa, such as *doubt, litre, comic, fat, isolate, place, institution.*

Why not try exploring other areas—symbols from chemistry (re*fer*, Ca*na*da) and maths (ra*pid*), initials and abbreviations (s*tuc*k, ra*cial*) according to the background and interests of the group?

SWAPPED SYLLABLES

A proposes a polysyllabic word. **B** must change one of the syllables to make a new word, and so on round the circle, e.g. contain, con*tend*, *pre*tend, pre*fer*, pre*pare*, *com*pare.

TENNIS ELBOW FOOT

A says a word. Within a strict time limit (say three seconds), **B** must say a second word that connects with the first in some way. Then **C** offers a third word to connect with **B**'s word, and so on round the circle. At any point a player may challenge the connection of another player. E.g.

> **A:** *tennis*
> **B:** *elbow*   (*tennis elbow* is an illness)
> **C:** *foot*   (*elbow* and *foot* are parts of the body)
> **D:** *ball*   (*foot* + *ball* = *football*)
> **E:** *fall*   (*fall* rhymes with *ball*)
> **F:** *autumn*   (*Fall* is US synonym for *Autumn*)
> **A:** *hymn*   (the last *-n* of *hymn* and *autumn* is silent)

In each group, members decide on 'acceptable' connections.

**RHYMING
DEFINITIONS**

Each player in turn must think of a rhyming phrase and give a brief definition of it; the others must then try to guess the phrase, e.g. large hog (*big pig*), happy father (*glad dad*), false pain (*fake ache*), senior policeman (*top cop*). (We learnt this from Eugene Raudsepp: *Creative Growth Games*, Perigee Books/Putnam.)

F/3 Anagrams

LEVEL

Elementary to Advanced

TIME

20–30 minutes

PREPARATION

Make a set of 100 cards, each bearing one letter of the alphabet. For a fair draw (see Step 2 below), use the typesetter's ETAOIN SRHDLU distribution, which reflects the frequency of each letter in normal English texts, so that in the set of 100 cards, there will be 10 E's, 9 T's, 8 A's, etc., according to the following table:

E 10	T 9	A 8	O 8	I 7	N 7	S 6	R 6	H 5	L 4	D 4
U 3	C 3	P 2	F 2	M 2	W 2	Y 2	B 2	G 2	VKQXJZ 1	

Separate the vowels AEIOU (38 cards) and consonants (62 cards) into two piles and shuffle each.

IN CLASS

1 Choose two teams, each of four members, and have them sit at the front of the class. Choose also a chairman, a secretary, a caller, and one or more judges.

2 Give the caller the two piles of shuffled Vowel and Consonant Cards. The first player in team **A** is invited to choose nine letters. S/he specifies whether each letter is a vowel or a consonant, and the caller draws the card from the appropriate pile, calling out the letter to the secretary as s/he does so. The secretary then writes the letter clearly on the board.

3 When all nine letters are on the board, the team **A** player, and his or her opposite number in team **B**, have 30 seconds to write down the longest word they can, using only those letters. Each letter may be used once only in the word.

4 Players are awarded points according to the length of their words, if correct: 3 points for a three-letter word, 4 for a four-letter word, and so on. Words may be challenged, and referred to the arbiter(s), who should have dictionaries.

5 The game continues until all the team members have drawn letters. The winning team is the one with the most points.

Acknowledgement
This type of game is traditional. The version described here derives from the Channel Four TV game 'Conundrum'.

F/4 Storyboard

The following exercise gives practice in relating words to context. It was originally devised as a computer game, but, with a little preparation by the teacher, works even better on the blackboard.

LEVEL

Elementary to Advanced

TIME

20–30 minutes

PREPARATION

Choose a short text, preferably containing not too much new lexical material for the class. Write it out clearly on cards measuring 20×15 cm, one word to a card, so that each word is clearly visible to the whole class. On the back of each card write the same word very small.

IN CLASS

1 Stick the cards to the wall or blackboard in the correct text sequence, with the large-print side hidden.

2 Tell the class that there is a text on the blackboard which they will have to uncover, one word at a time. Ask them to shout out any words that come to mind: if you hear any of the words in the text, reverse the corresponding card immediately, using the small-print words as a reminder.

3 From chance beginnings the text will gradually appear, as more and more context becomes available to the students.

VARIATION

In a large class, you may find it easier to allow only a small group to come to the front to participate actively in the exercise.

Acknowledgement
John Higgins and Graham Davies: *Storyboard* (Wida Software 1982). This activity is proposed as a grammar exercise in M. Rinvolucri: *Grammar Games* (CUP 1985).

Exercises F/5 to F/15 encourage the students to become familiar with the uses and functions of a dictionary in a more or less light-hearted way.

F/5 Word dip

LEVEL

Elementary to Advanced

TIME

15–25 minutes

PREPARATION

Ensure that you have sufficient monolingual dictionaries available: one for each group of 2–4 players. Any monolingual dictionary will do, though for more advanced students the various learners' dictionaries may be less stimulating. Pocket dictionaries will not be adequate.

1 Ask the students to form groups of 2–4 players each. Make sure each group has a dictionary.

2 Explain or demonstrate the game, then ask the groups to play one complete round. The game goes like this:

a. Player **A** opens the dictionary at random.

b. S/he chooses an unknown word defined on the pages open and tells the other player(s) what it is. (It may be helpful to insist that **A** both pronounces the word and spells it out. **A** may also give other information, such as part of speech, but *not* meaning.)

c. The other players then question **A** on the meaning of the word. **A** may answer only *yes* or *no*.

d. **A** scores a point if no one guesses the meaning within, say, twenty questions. Otherwise the first person to guess the meaning gets the point.

Two or three rounds should be the maximum to sustain interest: if the students wish to continue, then repeat the game on a later occasion.

F/6 Call my bluff

LEVEL

Intermediate to Advanced

TIME

20–30 minutes

PREPARATION

Ensure that you have sufficient monolingual dictionaries available: one for each group of 3–4 players. Any monolingual dictionary will do, though for more advanced students the various learners' dictionaries may be less stimulating. Pocket dictionaries will not be adequate.

IN CLASS

1 Ask the students to form groups of 3–4 players each. Make sure each group has a dictionary.

2 Ask each group to select one word from the dictionary which they think will be unknown to the rest of the class.

3 Within each group one player should then write down a correct definition of the word (copied or adapted from the dictionary), while the other players write down *false* definitions.

4 Pair the groups to play the game:

a. Group **A** tells Group **B** the word they have chosen.

b. Each player in Group **A** reads out his or her definition of the word.

c. Each player in Group **B** judges which definition is correct, and which are bluffs: they then try to achieve consensus among themselves.

d. The members of Group **B** announce their choice to Group **A**.

e. Group **B** now tells Group **A** the word they have chosen, and the game continues.

While groups **A** and **B** are playing together, **C** and **D**, **E** and **F**, etc. are doing the same thing.

F/7 From word to word

Intermediate to Advanced

15–25 minutes

Ensure that you have sufficient monolingual dictionaries available for each student: it may be more interesting if you provide a selection of different dictionaries. Pocket dictionaries will not be adequate. You are strongly advised to try the exercise out yourself, in some language other than English or your mother tongue, before introducing it in the classroom.

1 Ask the students to work individually: give each student a dictionary, or make sure s/he has brought one to class.

2 Write up a word on the blackboard: choose one which will produce a rich set of paraphrases/synonyms.

3 Ask the students to look up in the dictionary the word on the board and to read through the definition(s). Then ask them to choose one of the words in the definition and to look that up.

4 Ask the students to continue in this way until they have looked up, say, a dozen words. At each stage they should write down the word they look up.

5 Ask them to form pairs and compare their lists.

Starting from the headword *plant*, one person produced this list:

plant → *vegetable* → *organism* → *structure* → *framework* → *skeleton* → *bone* → *bobbin* → *reel* → *cylinder* → *tubular* → chamber

1 After working through steps 1–4 above, ask the students to link the words in their list into a paragraph or short story.

2 Build some or all words noted down into a picture.

3 Ask the students to use the technique above to 'quarry' words relating to a particular subject or theme (e.g. words needed in writing a description, words used by policemen).

F/8 Translation game

LEVEL	Elementary to Advanced
TIME	15–20 minutes
PREPARATION	Ensure that each member of the group possesses or has access to a good bilingual dictionary (English–mother-tongue/mother-tongue–English). Pocket dictionaries will not be adequate.
IN CLASS	1 Ask the students to work individually. 2 Write up an English word on the blackboard: choose one which will produce a rich set of translations. 3 Ask the students to look up in the dictionary the word on the board and to read through the translation(s) given. Then ask them to choose one mother-tongue word that translates the English word and to look that up in the mother-tongue–English section of the dictionary. They should then choose one of the English translations offered for that word and repeat the process. 4 Ask the students to continue in this way until they have looked up, say, a dozen words. At each stage they should write down the word they look up.
EXAMPLE	Working with a German–English dictionary, one person produced this list:

BAG → *Sack* → SACK → *Laufpass* → DISMISSAL → *Entlassung* → RELEASE → *Befreiung* → DELIVERANCE → *Rettung* → SALVAGE → *Bergung* → SHELTERING → *Zuflucht* → REFUGE

F/9 Crazy text

LEVEL	Beginner to Advanced
TIME	15 minutes
PREPARATION	Choose a short text (3–4 lines only). (See example below.)
IN CLASS	1 Tell the class that they are going to make certain alterations to the words in a text that you will give them: the alterations will be to nouns (or to verbs, or to adjectives) only. 2 Give out the texts to each student or pair of students. 3 Tell them to look up in turn each noun (or verb or adjective) in their dictionary (bilingual or monolingual) and to choose one word from the

translation/definition. They should then look this word up and choose any noun (or verb or adjective) *on the same page* and replace the original text word by this new word, making any minor adjustments needed to grammar (articles, concord, etc.).

4 Finally, students can be asked to compare their versions of the text.

EXAMPLE

Original text:

A Russian who made a winter hat from the fur of a neighbour's sheepdog was sentenced to three years' gaol by a court in the Tyla area, south of Moscow, according to the Soviet newspaper 'Trud'. (The Guardian 29.8.83)

Replacing nouns only in the way described above, using the *Oxford Advanced Learner's Dictionary of Current English*:

winter	: *season*	→	*seat*
hat	: *covering*	→	*cover*
fur	: *hair*	→	*half*
neighbour	: *person*	→	*personage*
sheepdog	: *shepherd*	→	*sheet*
gaol	: *prison*	→	*privation*
court	: *justice*	→	*juvenile*
area	: *region*	→	*register*
newspaper	: *publication*	→	*pudding*

gives:

A Russian who made a seat cover from the half of a personage's sheet was sentenced to three years' privation by a juvenile in the Tyla register, south of Moscow, according to the Soviet pudding 'Trud'.

F/10 Expansions

LEVEL

Elementary to Advanced

TIME

20–30 minutes

IN CLASS

1 Take a short quotation, proverb, etc. Put it on the blackboard and ask the students to copy it down at the top of a blank sheet of paper.

2 Working alone or in pairs, the students should
   a. copy out keywords from the original phrase;
   b. under each keyword, write a short dictionary definition of that word;
   c. making necessary grammatical alterations, link the definitions to produce a new sentence or sequence of sentences;
   d. copy out the keywords from the new sentence(s);
   e. repeat steps (b)–(c) for as long as is wished.

EXAMPLE

Look before you leap. Collins's *English Learner's Dictionary* produced the following:

look	before	leap
turn one's eyes towards	at an earlier time	jump

Turn your eyes towards me. At an earlier time I jumped.

turn	eyes	earlier	time	jumped
change	parts with which	nearer the	occasion	moved
	people see	beginning		quickly

Change the parts with which people see: nearer the beginning, the occasion moved quickly.

VARIATIONS

1 Use a bilingual dictionary, translating alternately back and forth.

2 Try the 'consequences' treatment (see D/14), passing the folded paper round a circle of 4–6 students at each stage.

Acknowledgement
This exercise was suggested in Oulipo: *La littérature potentielle* (Gallimard 1973) pages 123–32.

F/11 Definitions

One way of getting students to understand the uses (and limitations) of dictionary definitions is to get them to write their own . . .

LEVEL

Elementary to Advanced

TIME

15–25 minutes

IN CLASS

1 Ask the students, in groups of 3–4, to invent interesting-sounding words. Tell them not to worry about meaning at this stage.

2 Ask the students to work alone to produce definitions of the words invented.

3 In the original groups of 3–4, the students compare definitions.

VARIATION

To give more shape to the exercise (at the risk of limiting experiment and imagination), specify a context for their neologisms: e.g. 'new scientific words', 'green-sounding words', 'advertiser's words'.

F/12 Write yourself in

LEVEL   **Elementary to Advanced**

TIME   **10–15 minutes**

PREPARATION   From a text or other current source of vocabulary, select (or ask the students to select) 6–12 words.

IN CLASS   1 Ask the students, working individually, to look up each of the words in their dictionaries. When they have read the entry and any example sentences given, they should construct example sentences for that word which include their own names, or references to themselves.

2 In small groups, the students compare their example sentences.

VARIATION   This exercise can easily be adapted as a pair exercise by asking the pairs to write sentences that apply to both members, e.g.

> veal: *We are both opposed to the production of white veal.*

F/13 Word-building

LEVEL   **Intermediate to Advanced**

TIME   **20–30 minutes**

IN CLASS   1 Put up the following on the blackboard:

> *in-   re-*
>
> *un-   -tion   -less*
>
> *-ness   -er*

2 Ask the class to suggest words that contain these elements, and then to brainstorm other prefixes and suffixes.

3 Invite the students, individually or in pairs, to invent words of their own containing the brainstormed elements, and then to use dictionaries to confirm their speculations.

F/14 Propaganda

LEVEL Elementary to Advanced

TIME 20–30 minutes

IN CLASS 1 Give out the following text:

2 Ask the students, in pairs or small groups, to write one of the following:

– a similar advertisement with dictionary entries to persuade the public that not to buy a certain item, e.g. caviare, classifies them as poor;
– an advertisement to persuade owners of micro-computers that they are old-fashioned if they don't buy a disk-drive;
– an advertisement to recruit boys into the army, on the grounds that you are not manly until you have shot a reasonable bag of people.

F/15 Improve your dictionary

LEVEL

Elementary to Advanced

TIME

15–20 minutes in the first class, **20–30 minutes** in the second

IN CLASS

1 Put the students in groups of 4–6. Ask each group to brainstorm and note down ways in which dictionaries could be improved, or made more useful. Stress that at this stage any idea, however crazy, should be noted down.

2 After 5–10 minutes, ask the groups to stop and to go back over the ideas they have noted down, and to select one of the best for development.

IN THE NEXT CLASS

Ask each group to produce a sample page of their new-style dictionary. If possible, have copies made of each group's work for circulation around the class.

OVER THE REST OF THE COURSE

Ask the students to develop and keep their own personal dictionaries/vocabulary books, incorporating any of the ideas suggested.

F/16 Translation Reversi

The old game of 'Reversi' (or 'Otello') is undergoing a revival at present on home micro-computers. A simple board and some pieces of card, however, are all that are needed to play the game—and to turn it into a vocabulary exercise.

LEVEL

Elementary to Advanced

TIME

20–30 minutes

STRAIGHT REVERSI

1 The traditional game is played by two players (White and Black) with 64 counters on an 8 × 8 squared board (a chess-board is ideal). Counters are white on one side and black on the other.

2 Each player in turn places a counter on the board, with her or his own colour uppermost. A capture is made when one has placed a piece at each end of a line of opposing pieces (row, column, or diagonal): the captured pieces remain in place but are turned over to reverse their colours.

3 In the first four moves the four centre squares are filled; thereafter, each move must be a capture: if a player cannot make a capture, s/he loses that turn.

4 The game ends when neither player has a legal move and/or the board is full. The winner is the player with the most pieces on the board at the end of the game.

**TRANSLATION
REVERSI**

This is played in exactly the same way as the traditional game, but with a few extra rules:

1 Small pieces of card are used instead of counters: on one side of each card is written a word or phrase in English, on the other an appropriate translation into the mother tongue. Instead of 'White' and 'Black', one player is 'English', the other 'Mother Tongue'.

2 Before being allowed to capture a single opposing piece, the player must be able to translate the word on it before completing the move. In capturing longer lines of pieces, s/he must translate at least two words in the capture string *before* moving.

Sources for the words and phrases used in the game could include current topic or text material, revision material, and problems thrown up by students' work.

VARIATIONS

1 The game may be shortened by using a 6 × 6 board (36 cards) or 7 × 7 board (49 cards).

2 Instead of translations, other paired items can be used: synonyms, antonyms, word + definition, orthographic/phonemic spelling, etc.

3 Although, when introducing the game, it may be simpler to use materials produced by the teacher, the activity has greater effect when the students produce materials for themselves or for each other.

Section G
Revision exercises

Traditionally, revision has been much more on most teachers' maps than other aspects of vocabulary work dealt with in this book: a colleague in Cambridge starts each morning on her intensive courses by asking students to close their eyes and think back over what they learnt the previous day . . .

A note on notebooks

Many of the exercises that follow should be done in the students' vocabulary notebooks. In this way learners will have a powerful record of the exercises they have done with and around new lexis. Many activities here aim, for example, to improve the *visual quality* of notebooks, to go beyond the monotonous column of bilingual pairs:

Frau – *woman*
und – *and*
Stuhl – *chair*

A ground plan of your home with the words you are learning written all over it is a lot more memorable than this (see G/5).

The vocabulary notebook may well be a sort of history of the language class: students can write personal notes about the circumstances of learning as well as the apparent 'content' of the lesson. From a Greek student, for example, we might have the following page:

ghost (phantasma)	*Got a good letter from home today.*
conviction (pepithisis)	*The teacher is looking out of the window.*
´politics	*It's a Greek word—I got the English stress wrong again!*
metaphor	*Makes me think of moving house.*

Not everybody is highly visual

The emphasis in this book and particularly this section is mainly on the visual channel of perception. The balance is only partly redressed in G/9 and G/10, where we address those whose memory and imagination favour the auditory channel. What, though, of touch? Much more thought needs to be given to the relation between memorability and the senses. Those interested in this might like to read Richard Bandler and John Grinder: *The Structure of Magic*, 2 vols (Science and Behaviour Books, Palo Alto 1975).

G/1 Open categorization

LEVEL   **Beginner to Advanced**

TIME   **15–20 minutes**

IN CLASS   **1** Write the words to be reviewed on the board.

2 Invite the students, working individually, to categorize the words into more than two groups. The way they do this is for them to choose: the look of the words on the page, associations with the words, the sounds of the words, idea groupings, etc. Do not tell the students how to categorize: let them find out for themselves.

3 Ask the students to give each of their categories a heading.

4 Go round the class, asking some of the students to read out their headings and the words in the corresponding categories. Do not reward or censure students by your facial expression and tone of voice for the way they have categorized: be as neutral as you can and say as little as possible.

NB: If you are working with beginners, all the language they use in performing the categorization task will be mother-tongue.

Acknowledgement
We learnt this technique from Caleb Gattegno's Silent Way. For more about his work, see his book, *The Common Sense of Teaching Foreign Languages* (New York: Educational Solutions 1976).

G/2 Guided categorization

We have found it useful in class to 'pervert' Gattegno's idea of open categorization in a number of ways, as, after a while, students get into a non-creative routine when asked simply to categorize. Here we present half a dozen ways of guiding the categorization process in interesting and provocative ways. All are intended to help students retain lexis they have recently met. Much more important than this, however, is what they learn about their fellow learners in the sharing that occurs round the words worked on. The new light in which people can see each other provides a new context of learning, beyond the simple linguistic 'context'.

LEVEL   **Beginner to Advanced**

TIME   **15–20 minutes**

A. NICE WORDS VERSUS NASTY WORDS

1 Give the students the words to be reviewed and ask them each to pick three they like and three they don't. Give them time to think.

2 Put up two headings on the board: *Nice words* and *Nasty words*. Ask each student to write up *one* of her or his nice words and *one* nasty word.

3 When everybody has two words on the board, invite people to explain why they like or dislike particular words. Do not gloss or comment yourself: don't give or withhold approval. By keeping quiet you will help the students to talk.

EXAMPLE

In one group the review words were:

viaduct	*ambulance*	*to lower*	*motorway*
plunge	*jack-knife*	*to volunteer*	*hair-raising* *jelly*
windscreen	*intensive*		

Here are some of the things different students said about some of the words:

ambulance: 'I used to be a nurse, and an ambulance coming meant more work. I don't like the word.'

intensive: 'I don't like it because the *-nt-* is too hard to say correctly.'

jelly: 'I like it. The sound is right.'

windscreen: 'I don't like it because I learnt it last term and can't remember it.'

VARIATION

The exercise above can be adapted to run over the course of a whole term:

1 Get a large sheet of card to hang on your classroom wall. Find a closed box and make a slot in the top: these will become permanent classroom fixtures. Have Blu-Tack handy.

2 Invite students to stick on the large sheet any words they like, or words that interest them: these may be single words written on slips of paper, cuttings from newspaper headlines or advertisements, etc. Ask them to 'throw away' in the box any words they don't like, or can't or don't want to remember, or which confuse or bother them. Tell them they can do this whenever they like during the course, and that periodically there will be a session in which they can explain why they put the words on the board or in the box, while others comment or make suggestions.

3 From time to time, hold comment sessions: let the students introduce their own words first, followed by comments from others. Try to keep in the background as far as possible and let the students run their own session.

Acknowledgement
We should like to thank Marilyn Spaventa, who used this technique with classes on Pilgrims summer courses.

B. OTHER SUBJECTIVE CATEGORIES

Using the methodology suggested in (A), you can ask the students to work on contrastive categories of many different sorts, e.g.

very English words	not very English words
new words	old words
me-connected words	separate-from-me words
high words	low words
past words	future words

C. WORDS AND SHAPES

1 Put up on the board the following shapes:

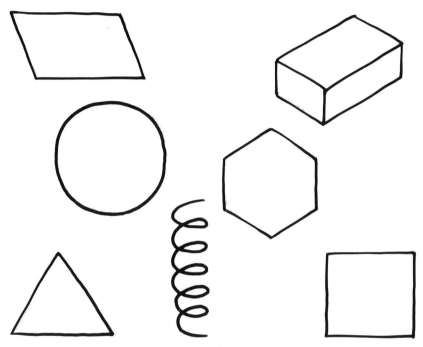

2 Ask the students to copy the shapes into their notebooks and then associate the words to be reviewed with the shapes. They may, of course, link a given word with more than one shape.

3 Pair the students and let them explain their word–shape associations.

D. WORDS AND COUNTRIES

1 Ask each student to jot down the name of a country s/he has enjoyed visiting or would like to visit.

2 Have them draw maps of these countries on the blackboard. (Strict accuracy is not important.)

3 Ask them to write down the names of the various countries across the top of a piece of paper, and then to rule the paper into columns, each with a country as a heading.

4 Put up your list of words and ask the students to write them in one or other column according to the associations they feel between their words and the countries.

5 Ask them to explain their associations to their neighbours.

EXAMPLE

In one class the list of words under review was:

shed	translucent	corrugated	hefty	staple	loop
rack	hinge	hook	lethal	draughty	pail	suck
drain	goat

One student produced these associations:

Romania	Mongolia	Denmark	Wales	USA	Tanzania
shed	*translucent*			*lethal*	*draughty*
pail		*hinge*		*drain*	*corrugated*
suck		*rack*		*hefty*	
goat					
No associations: *staple/loop/hook*					

E. WORDS AND COLOURS

1 Ask each student to write down six colours in order of preference, ranging from most liked to most disliked. (For this exercise black and white are colours.)

2 Put a set of words on the board and ask the students to associate the words with the colours. They should do this individually in writing.

3 Ask individual students to tell the class which colours they assigned to different words and why.

G/3 Guess who

LEVEL

Intermediate to Advanced

TIME

15–30 minutes

PREPARATION

Make a list of 30–40 words that the students have found hard in a topic area and write them on a page in disorder. Put the words into idea groups: not from your own point of view, but from that of some stereotypic individual. Repeat with a different stereotype. Make one copy of each of these three lists for each member of the class. (See the example overleaf, where the topic area is *babies*: Person **A** could be a rather baby-centred, middle-aged woman, while Person **B** could be a baby.)

IN CLASS

1 Give out the disordered word sheets. Ask the students to check the meanings of any words they can't remember.

2 Give out the **Person A** and **Person B** idea groupings. Ask the students to work in threes and decide what sort of people **A** and **B** might be, and to describe their attitudes.

3 Once you feel that most groups have reached some sort of conclusion, ask one person from each group to go to the next group to report.

BABY-SITTER   PAEDIATRICIAN   SIBLING   NURSE

COT   FUNNY   JEALOUSY   TENDERNESS

PROTECTION   BATTERED BABY   BUNK-BED   BOTTLE-FEED

FREUD   NOISE   GAME   BIB   LABOUR

TOYS   PLASTIC PANTS   BARREN

BREAST-FEED   DELIVERY   CONFINEMENT

RELAXATION   PREGNANCY   PATERNITY LEAVE   DAUGHTER   CRÈCHE

CRY   AFFECTION   FANTASY   NAPPY   CHORTLE

Person A

good things	neutral things	bad things
bib	labour	jealousy
protection	funny	baby-sitter
tenderness	Freud	nurse
paediatrician	sibling	crèche
cot	noise	barren
affection		relaxation
confinement		paternity leave
pregnancy		
daughter		
breast-feed		
nappy		
chortle	*impossible things*	
cry	battered baby	
delivery	bottle-feed	
bunk-bed		
toys		
plastic pants		

Person B

words I know nothing about

	'now' words	'future' words
Freud	bib	crèche
sibling	affection	jealousy
bunk-bed	plastic pants	game
battered baby	protection	toys
barren	cot	baby-sitter
daughter	breast-feed	paediatrician
funny	chortle	
bottle-feed	tenderness	
paternity leave	relaxation	*'past' words*
	noise	labour
	fantasy	pregnancy
	nappy	confinement
	cry	nurse

G/4 Word grids

In this exercise we have taken the mechanism of componential analysis from the linguists via its use in therapy. In the therapeutic use and in ours, the grid is being used to get people to express and become aware of their subjectivity.

LEVEL

Intermediate to Advanced

TIME

15–20 minutes

IN CLASS

1 Put the grid below on the board and ask the students to copy it into their notebooks:

valuable	___	___	___	___	___	worthless
shallow	___	___	___	___	___	deep
slow	___	___	___	___	___	fast
active	___	___	___	___	___	passive
small	___	___	___	___	___	large
clean	___	___	___	___	___	dirty
weak	___	___	___	___	___	strong
tasty	___	___	___	___	___	distasteful
relaxed	___	___	___	___	___	tense
cold	___	___	___	___	___	hot

2 Write the words to be revised on the board and ask the students, working individually, to choose six words and decide where each of them should go on the grid. If one of the words to be revised were *consistency*, for example, a student's grid might look like this:

valuable	X	___	___	___	___	worthless
shallow	___	___	___	X	___	deep
slow	___	___	X	___	___	fast
active	___	X	___	___	___	passive

This student thinks consistency is a valuable quality that probably indicates depth. Speed seems unimportant, but it takes an active stance to be consistent . . .

3 Pair the students and ask them to explain their grids to their partners.

VARIATION

Instead of placing the words to be reviewed on a word grid, use them as the 'poles' in the grid, and place *yourself* on it. Suppose you're just starting Turkish and want to revise the words below: place yourself in the appropriate space between each pair of poles:

ev (house)	___	___	___	___	___	adan (man)
kiz (girl)	___	___	___	___	___	orman (forest)
sehir (city)	___	___	___	___	___	koy (village)
göz (eye)	___	___	___	___	___	bas (head)
deniz (sea)	___	___	___	___	___	açiktim (I'm hungry)

G/5 Lexical furniture

LEVEL

Elementary to Advanced

TIME

15–20 minutes

IN CLASS

1 Ask each student to draw a ground plan of his or her house/flat/home/room.

2 Put up on the blackboard a set of twenty or so words for revision.

3 Working on their own, the students should then place the words in appropriate positions in their living place.

4 In pairs, they look at each other's placings and discuss them.

EXAMPLE

In one class, a girl put *perplexed* in the garage because her mother could never understand why her car would not start; *furious* outside the house because her parents would not allow expressions of anger inside; *do an experiment* in the kitchen . . .

NOTE

Placing words or ideas to be remembered in your house or along your high street is one of the oldest memory techniques known. It was this method that was used by Shereshevskii, the prodigious memory man, studied in *The Mind of a Mnemonist*, by A. R. Luria (Penguin 1975).

VARIATIONS

1 Each student draws a clockface: the words to be reviewed are placed on the clockface according to temporal associations.

2 Ask the students to write down twenty times of day when regular things happen, e.g.

8.15 *Wife leaves for work.*
8.30 *Postman comes.*
9.10 *I finish washing up the breakfast dishes.*

They should then write the words to be reviewed alongside the times, as they think appropriate.

3 Ask each student to draw a map of their district, and to mark on it one or more of the routes they regularly follow (e.g. to work, to school, to a friend's house). On this map they should then place the words to be reviewed.

G/6 Leaping words

LEVEL

Beginner to Advanced

TIME

10–15 minutes

IN CLASS

1 Ask the students to choose 15 words they find hard to remember from the last few pages of their vocabulary notebooks. They should

check them with a neighbour or you and/or a dictionary.

2 They should now rewrite the words, using calligraphic artifice to bring out the meanings.

3 Ask them to get up and move around the room to show their designs to as many people as possible, explaining why they see particular words thus.

EXAMPLE

In one group *spit* was written

by one student, and *jealousy* as a spiral by another:

Acknowledgement
We first learnt this technique from Michael Legutke of Giessen University.

G/7 Find the word a picture

LEVEL

Beginner to Advanced

TIME

20–40 minutes

PREPARATION

Select 60 words that need revising from the work done during previous classes. Put each word on a separate card. Select 100 pictures or parts of pictures from magazines.

IN CLASS

1 Give out the word cards to the students: if you have twenty students, each will get three cards; if thirty, each will get two.

2 Spread the magazine pictures on flat surfaces round the room. Ask the students to get up and circulate. Their task is to find pictures that somehow match each of their words. It is up to them to decide how. You should be available to help students who don't remember their words.

3 Ask the students to explain to each other how they have matched their words and pictures. Each should talk to at least five other people.

EXAMPLES

Here are some examples of links that students found between words and pictures, and the explanations they gave:

Words	Pictures	Explanations
rage	a policeman violently carrying off a small child	'It makes me angry.'
a well	a man drowning under a bridge	
hostility	people in a poor quarter jeering at an armed policeman	
forger	plush, shiny cushions on a settee	'Because the leather looks false.'
guilt	a girl running across a street	'Because she feels guilt.'
sprocket	mother holding two young children	'They look as close as a sprocket is to a wheel.'

G/8 Rhyming review

LEVEL

Elementary to Advanced

TIME

20–30 minutes

PREPARATION

Choose 10–15 words and put each on a separate card.

IN CLASS

1 Each student is given a word card and asked to think of a word that rhymes with it. Suppose the word on the card is *mess*. The student might choose *guess*. The student then says: 'The word on my card rhymes with *guess*.'

2 Other students in the group then have to discover what the word on the first student's card is. They do this by asking questions, e.g.

Student A:	*Is it something a girl wears?*
Card Student:	*No, it isn't 'dress'.*
Student B:	*Is it something people who live in cities feel a lot?*
Card Student:	*No, not 'stress'.*
Student C:	*Is it what a priest does?*
Card Student:	*No, not 'bless'.*

3 Redistribute the cards, and play the game again.

Acknowledgement
The idea for this activity came from Hurwitz and Goddard: *Games to Improve Your Child's English* (Kaye and Ward 1972).

G/9 Draw the word

LEVEL	**Beginner to Advanced**
TIME	**5 minutes** in the first class, **15–20 minutes** in the second
PREPARATION	Choose the words you want the students to review. There is no reason why these should be only ones that are easily represented in drawing.
IN CLASS	Put the words on the board, then tell the students to draw a picture for each word as homework.
IN THE NEXT CLASS	Ask the students to work in pairs, simultaneously, showing their drawings to each other and explaining why they feel the drawings fit the words.

EXAMPLE

interregnum: One king dead on the ground and another alive, about to be crowned.

replacement: One person handing a bag to another.

to receive: A bricklayer receiving a brick from a helper.

to reach: A person trying to get something from the top of a high cupboard.

to emphasize: A teacher at a blackboard, underlining two words.

desire: A cyclist gazing at a van. (The student explained that this was the cyclist's desire for the van.)

exclusive: A house surrounded by high walls and locked gates.

skill: A potter making a vase at a wheel.

observation: A fire-watching tower in a forest.

to develop: A child at various stages of growth from infancy.

VARIATION

1 Write the words on the blackboard in arbitrary pairs.

2 Ask the students, working individually, to draw pictures linking the words in each pair.

3 *Either* ask the students to show their pictures to one or two neighbours and explain the links shown; *or* form groups of 4–5 students. In each group, all the pictures should be pooled, and one by one individuals should take a picture from the pool and try to guess the words represented and the links between them.

G/10 Pegwords

LEVEL

Beginner to Advanced

TIME

10 minutes at the start of the class and **5 minutes** at the end

IN CLASS

1 At the very start of your lesson, write the following on the board:

one = bun	*two = shoe*	*three = tree*	*four = door*
five = hive	*six = sticks*	*seven = heaven*	*eight = gate*
nine = wine	*ten = hen*		

2 Explain that you are going to show them a technique for remembering sequences of unrelated items. Each of the 'pegwords' above is associated (and rhymes) with an item's position in a list. They must then devise an image linking the 'pegword' and the item. For example, if item 8 was the word 'cat' then one might imagine a scene in which a cat was walking across the top of a field gate. The song 'Knick Knack Paddywhack' can be used to learn the 'pegwords'.

3 Write the word list on the blackboard. Number each item 1–10.

4 Ask the students, working individually, to imagine a scene or situation linking each word with its appropriate 'pegword'. Allow no writing.

5 Clean the blackboard, and get on with some other, unrelated piece of work.

6 At the end of the lesson, ask the students to write down the original list of words from memory, *in the correct sequence*.

Acknowledgement
We found this technique in A. Baddeley: *Your Memory* (Penguin 1983) and heard about its use in class from Antonia Paín of Caceres University.

G/11 Matching words

LEVEL

Elementary to Advanced

TIME

15–30 minutes

PREPARATION

Select not more than thirty words that need reviewing. Put each one on a separate card. For each word find a synonym, opposite, dictionary definition, or 'groping definition' and put one of these on a card, so that you end up with thirty cards that match the thirty word cards. Here are examples for four words:

word cards	matching cards	
tact	*diplomacy*	(synonym)
guts	*cowardice*	(opposite)
elegance	*the quality of being refined or graceful*	(dictionary definition)
honesty	*it begins with 'h'—you can trust someone who has it—they won't lie to you*	(groping definition)

IN CLASS

1 Give each student one or two of the word cards and one or two of the matching cards (depending on class size) and ask them to get up and mill around the room trying to find cards to match their own. Ask them to note down who has the cards corresponding to theirs, and what is on them. (This reduces chaos.)

2 Ask a student to call out one of his or her words: the person with the matching card then calls out the matching word or definition. This goes on until all the cards have been matched.

VARIATION

The preparation outlined above takes quite a bit of time. Why do it yourself? Simply choose the words you want revised (or ask the students to choose) and ask a more advanced group to provide the synonyms, opposites, and definitions to put on card. They will be delighted to know their work is being put to a directly practical use.

Acknowledgement
Mike Lavery gave us the outline of this exercise. The idea of using 'groping definitions' has been used in Berer and Rinvolucri: *Mazes* (Heinemann 1981).

G/12 Gift words

LEVEL

Beginner to Advanced

TIME

20 minutes

IN CLASS

1 Ask the students to pick out twenty words they feel need reviewing from recent work and to check that they know what they mean.

2 Tell them to put the words each on a slip of paper, and to write on each slip the name of a person in the group for whom the word would be an appropriate gift.

3 Everyone now gets up and mills around, giving the words away. If the receiver of a word does not understand it, the giver should explain the meaning, and the reason for the gift.

VARIATION

Half the class sit with their word slips spread out in front of them. The other half move round taking the words they feel they would like, and explaining why.

Acknowledgement
This exercise is a transposition of an activity used in therapy and proposed by Ted Saretsky in *Active Techniques and Group Therapy* (Jason Aronson 1977).

G/13 Forced choice

LEVEL

Elementary to Advanced

TIME

15–25 minutes

PREPARATION

Choose half a dozen pairs of words from a vocabulary area to be revised, so that there is an opposition within each pair. If, for example, you want students to review 'water words', you might choose these pairs:

spring	:	*well*
estuary	:	*waterfall*
drowning	:	*floating*
starfish	:	*whale*
lake	:	*river*
sprinkler	:	*goggles*

IN CLASS

1 Get all the students standing in the middle of the room. Tell them you are going to offer them a choice: they are going to have to choose which thing they think they are most like. If you are working with *water* you might say:

'People who think they are like a *spring* must go to that end of the room. People who think they are like a *well* must go to the other end of the room.'

Oblige any fence-sitters to decide and choose one end of the room.

2 Now ask the people to talk to their neighbours in *pairs* and explain why they chose as they did. Insist that they work in pairs, not clusters of three or more.

3 Ask students from one end of the room to go over and talk to the people who made the opposite choice.

4 Repeat steps 1, 2, and 3 with a new pair of words.

Acknowledgement
We learnt this technique from S. B. Simon, Howe and Kirschenbaum: *Values Clarification* (Hart Co., New York).

G/14 Question and answer

LEVEL Elementary to Advanced

TIME 15–25 minutes

PREPARATION Select 30–40 words that need reviewing. Prepare cards with ten words on each. Every student will need to be given one ten-word card.

IN CLASS 1 Pair the students. Give each person a card and ensure that partners have different cards.

2 Student **A** must not show his or her card to student **B**. Student **A** looks at the first word on the card and asks **B** a question aimed at getting **B** to say the word. If **A**'s question does not elicit from **B** the word on **A**'s card, **A** fires more questions until **B** says the word. This is how it can go:

The first word on **A**'s card is *invasion*.

> **A:** *What did the Americans do to Vietnam?*
> **B:** *Bombed it?*
> **A:** *Yes . . . and what have the Israelis often done to Lebanon?*
> **B:** *Attacked it?*
> **A:** *What do you say when one country moves an army into another?*
> **B:** *It invades it.*
> **A:** *What's the noun for that?*
> **B:** *'Invasion'.*

3 **B** does the same to **A**. They alternate until all the words on both cards have been dealt with.

Acknowledgement
We found this technique in Byrne and Rixon (eds.): *Communication Games: ELT Guide 1* (NFER Publishing Co.).

G/15 Chain story

LEVEL Elementary to Advanced

TIME 15–20 minutes

PREPARATION Put the words you want the students to revise on separate cards. Choose as many words as students in the group + one.

IN CLASS 1 Give each student a word card. Ask them to check that they know the meaning of their words.

2 Get the students into groups of 8–10. Take the last word card yourself and start a story, using the word. Do not speak for more than 45 seconds.

3 Designate a person in each group to carry on the story, using their word. Each person must speak for about 45 seconds. Agree on a signal to show that the 45 seconds is up and that it is time for another student to take over the story. Each speaker is to designate the next speaker, until everyone has had a turn.

G/16 Words to story

LEVEL

Elementary to Advanced

TIME

20–30 minutes

PREPARATION

Choose 30–40 words that need revising.

IN CLASS

1 Write the words on the board. Ask the students to check any words they don't remember the meaning of.

2 Ask each student to pick 6–7 words from those on the board.

3 Each student then makes up a story (mentally, not on paper) suggested by the words s/he has chosen.

4 The students pair off and tell each other their stories, then explain how they chose those particular words.

G/17 Word rush

LEVEL

Beginner to Intermediate

TIME

10 minutes

PREPARATION

Put 20 words to be reviewed each on to a separate card.

IN CLASS

1 Divide the class into two teams, **A** and **B**. Have the two teams assemble at one end of the classroom. Go to the other end yourself.

2 Call out a member of each team and show them one word.

3 Each team member rushes back to his or her team and *draws* the word. S/he must *not* write, speak, gesture or whisper! The first team that recognizes the word from the drawing and shouts it out correctly gets a point.

Acknowledgement
The activity comes from Viola Spolin's gold-mine of drama ideas, *Improvisation for the Theatre* (Pitman 1963).

Bibliography

Learning: theory and practice

Sylvia Ashton-Warner *Teacher*. London: Secker and Warburg, 1963.
Experiences of a teacher in New Zealand, with remarkable insight
into children's motivations to learn.
A. Baddeley *Your Memory*. London: Penguin, 1983.
Ruth Gairns and Stuart Redman: *Working with Words*. Cambridge:
Cambridge University Press, 1986.
The first systematic theoretical treatment of vocabulary acquisition.
Caleb Gattegno *The Common Sense of Teaching Foreign Languages*.
New York: Education Solutions, 1976.
Paulo Freire *Cultural Action for Freedom*. London: Penguin, 1972.
The cultural and political power of words, in the context of adult
literacy programmes.
A. R. Luria *The Mind of a Mnemonist*. London: Penguin, 1975.
Earl Stevick *Memory, Meaning and Method*. Rowley, MA: Newbury
House, 1976.
Particularly good as a survey of current views on memory and
vocabulary retention.
Earl Stevick *A Way and Ways*. Rowley, MA: Newbury House, 1980.
An excellent survey of 'new' methods in language teaching.

Useful sources of exercise material

Virginia French Allen *Techniques in Vocabulary Teaching*. New York:
Oxford University Press, 1983.
One of the very few books to tackle vocabulary as a classroom
activity: conservative, but with several good ideas.
Richard Bandler and John Grinder *The Structure of Magic* (two
volumes). Palo Alto: Science and Behaviour Books, 1975.
Don Byrne and Shelagh Rixon *ELT Guide I: Communication Games*.
London: NFER/The British Council, 1979. Second edition:
NFER/Nelson/The British Council, 1982.
Christine Frank and Mario Rinvolucri *Grammar in Action*. Oxford:
Pergamon/Munich: Max Hueber 1983.
Awareness activities for grammar practice: many of the suggestions
can be adapted to vocabulary practice.
Hurwitz and Goddard *Games to Improve Your Child's English*.
London: Kaye and Ward, 1972.
Sue Jennings *Remedial Drama*. London: Pitman, 1973.
Mike Lavery 'Lead-ins and Fade-outs'. Unpublished manuscript.
John Morgan and Mario Rinvolucri *Once Upon a Time*. Cambridge:
Cambridge University Press, 1983.

Storytelling in the classroom, including a number of ideas for building stories from the word-level up.

Gertrude Moskowitz *Caring and Sharing in the Foreign Language Class*. Rowley, MA: Newbury House, 1978.
The classic humanistic activities book.

J. W. Pfeiffer and J. E. Jones (eds.) *Structured Experiences for Human Relations Training*. La Jolla, CA: University Associates, 1978.

Eugene Raudsepp *Creative Growth Games*. New York: Putnam, 1977.

Mario Rinvolucri *Grammar Games*. Cambridge: Cambridge University Press, 1985.
Includes a number of vocabulary-related games.

Ted Saretsky *Active Techniques and Group Therapy*. New York: Jason Aronson, 1977.
A valuable sourcebook for anyone involved in groups, not just therapists.

S. B. Simon, Howe and Kirschenbaum *Values Clarification*. New York: Hart, 1972.
Exercises to help students discover what they really believe.

Viola Spolin *Improvisation for the Theatre*.   London: Pitman, 1973.

Michael Swan and Catherine Walter *The Cambridge English Course*. Cambridge: Cambridge University Press, 1984/85.
A coursebook with strong emphasis on vocabulary acquisition.

Approaches to text work

Marge Berer and Mario Rinvolucri *Mazes*. London: Heinemann, 1981; Munich: Max Hueber, 1985.

Marge Berer and Mario Rinvolucri *Mazes II*. Canterbury: Pilgrims, 1981.
Non-linear text reading.

Anthony Burgess *A Clockwork Orange*. London: Penguin, 1962.
In which a hundred completely new words are learnt without effort.

Werner Lansburgh *Dear Doosie*. Frankfurt: Fischer, 1977.
An excellent and very witty mixed-language text.

Oulipo *La Littérature potentielle*. Paris: Gallimard, 1973.
A rich compendium of ideas for text creation.

Computer programs referred to in the text

John Higgins and Graham Davies *Storyboard* (second edition). London: Wida Software, 1985.
Guess the text: excellent for contextual and prediction work.

Chris Jones *Wordstore*. London: Wida Software, 1985.
Enables you to write and maintain your own dynamic dictionary.

Other titles in the Resource Books for Teachers series

Beginners, by Peter Grundy – provides over 100 original and communicative activities for teaching both absolute and 'false' beginners. Includes a section aimed at learners who do not know the Latin alphabet. (ISBN 0 19 437200 6)

CALL, by David Hardisty and Scott Windeatt – offers the teacher a bank of practical activities, based on communicative methodology, which make use of a variety of computer programs. (ISBN 0 19 437105 0)

Class Readers, by Jean Greenwood – practical advice and activities to develop extensive and intensive reading skills, listening activities, oral tasks, and both perceptive and literary skills. (ISBN 0 19 437103 4)

Classroom Dynamics, by Jill Hadfield – a practical book to help teachers maintain a good working relationship with their classes, and so promote effective learning. Includes activities for ice-breaking and fostering self-confidence, as well as a chapter on 'coping with crisis'. (ISBN 0 19 437096 8)

Cultural Awareness, by Barry Tomalin and Susan Stempleski – activities to increase cultural awareness and inter-cultural interaction among students, both challenging stereotypes and using cultural issues as a rich resource for language practice. (ISBN 0 19 437194 8)

Drama, by Charlyn Wessels – first-hand, practical advice on how to use drama to promote language acquisition, improve coursebook presentation, teach spoken communication skills and literature, and make language learning more creative and enjoyable. (ISBN 0 19 437097 6)

Grammar Dictation, by Ruth Wajnryb – also known as 'dictogloss', this technique improves students' understanding and use of grammar. By reconstructing texts, students find out more about how English works. (ISBN 0 19 437097 6)

Learner-based Teaching, by Colin Campbell and Hanna Kryszewska – contains over 70 language practice activities which unlock the wealth of knowledge that learners bring to the classroom. (ISBN 0 19 437163 8)

Literature, by Alan Maley and Alan Duff – an innovatory book on using literature for language practice. The activities can be used not only with the sample materials provided, but with materials of the teacher's own choice. (ISBN 0 19 437094 1)

Music and Song, by Tim Murphey – ideas for using all types of music and song in the classroom in lively and interesting ways. It shows teachers how 'tuning in' to their students' musical tastes can increase motivation and tap a rich vein of resources. (ISBN 0 19 437055 0)

Newspapers, by Peter Grundy – full of creative and original ideas for making effective use of newspapers in lessons. The activities are practical, need little teacher preparation, and can be applied to a wide range of articles and extracts. (ISBN 0 19 437192 6)

Project Work, by Diana L. Fried-Booth – provides practical resources for teachers who are interested in bridging the gap between the classroom and the outside world by integrating language learning with projects. (ISBN 0 19 437092 5)

Pronunciation, by Clemont Laroy – an innovative book which comes to grips with the underlying reasons behind poor pronunciation. Provides imaginative activities to build confidence and improve all aspects of pronunciation. (ISBN 0 19 437089 9)

Role Play, by Gillian Porter Ladousse – an ideal vehicle for developing fluency and integrating the four skills. Activities range from highly controlled conversations to improvised drama, and from simple dialogues to complex scenarios. (ISBN 0 19 437095 X)

Self-Access, by Susan Sheerin – is designed to help EFL and ESL teachers with the practicalities of setting up and managing self-access study facilities and so enable learning to continue independently of teaching. (ISBN 0 19 437099 2)

Storytelling with Children, by Andrew Wright – exploits children's natural affinity with stories by using them to motivate children to listen to English, become aware of its sound and feel, and understand language points. Includes over 30 stories and ideas for using any story in class. (ISBN 0 19 437202 2)

Translation, by Alan Duff – explores the role of translation in language learning and provides teachers with a wide variety of translation activities from many different subject areas. No specialist knowledge or previous experience of translation is required. (ISBN 0 19 437104 2)

Video, by Richard Cooper, Mike Lavery, and Mario Rinvolucri – a practical book which encourages students to explore the interaction between camera and image, and provides them with real tasks involving the language of perception, observation, and argumentation. (ISBN 0 19 437192 6)

Writing, by Tricia Hedge – an award-winning book which presents a wide range of writing tasks to improve learners' 'authoring' and 'crafting' skills, as well as guidance on student difficulties with writing. (ISBN 0 19 437098 4)

Young Learners, by Sarah Phillips – ideas and materials for a wide variety of language practice activities, including arts and crafts, games, storytelling, poems, and songs. The book also gives guidance to teachers new to teaching English to young learners. (ISBN 0 19 437195 6)